Fail Big.

More Bestselling Titles From Scott Allan

Empower Your Thoughts

Empower Your Deep Focus

Rejection Reset

Rejection Free

Relaunch Your Life

Drive Your Destiny

The Discipline of Masters

Do the Hard Things First

Undefeated

No Punches Pulled

Fail Big

Bite the Bullet

Supercharge Your Best Life

Built for Stealth

Visit author.to/ScottAllanBooks to follow Scott Allan and stay up to date on future book releases

FAIL

BIG

*Fail Your Way to Success and
Break All the Rules to Get There*

By Scott Allan

CONTENTS

JOIN THE COMMUNITY OF 30,000 LIFETIME LEARNERS!

Sign up today for my **free weekly newsletter** and receive instant access to **the <u>onboarding subscriber pack</u>** that includes:

The Fearless Confidence Action Guide: 9 Action Plans for Building Limitless Confidence and Achieving Sustainable Results!

The bestseller poster pack: A poster set of Scott Allan's bestselling books

The Zero Procrastination Blueprint: A Step-by-Step Blueprint to Turn Procrastination into Rapid Action Implementation!

Begin Your Journey and Make This Life Your Own.
Click Here to <u>Subscribe Today</u>, or scan the <u>QR code</u> below.

"Many of life's failures are people who did not realize how close they were to success when they gave up."

— **Thomas Edison**

The Fear of Falling Down

Most of us hate to fail. I've never come across anyone who actually said they enjoyed it or tried to fail with intention. We are so busy trying to succeed and get ahead in life that, who really thinks about failing?

Yet, the fear of failure is the #1 reason most people *do* fail.

When you do fail at something—you didn't complete the race, you got divorced within six months of marriage, or you just went bankrupt for the second time—it seems like everyone is looking at you. Judging you. Are they thinking, *What a loser?* They are likely thinking, *Better her than me.*

And, they would be right. Who wants to go through unnecessary hardship? Who wants to put in a lot of effort without that guarantee of making it work? Who wants to risk looking bad, or losing what they hold most valuable? Who wants to be the one singled out?

When you fail at something in life, it seems as if you become the center of attention. People start to talk about you. They point at you on the street and say things like, "Did you hear what happened to..."

Or is this all in your head? It's probably both. But do you know what. No matter what you are told, I believe most people look at someone else's failure as a warning: *If I do the same thing, that could be me.* We learn and record what happens. But when you finally succeed, everyone wants to know, *"How did you do that?"*

Your failure becomes a success story. Your hardship turns into a series of lessons for people to model and succeed themselves. It transforms your biggest struggle into your greatest victory.

By avoiding the pitfalls of looking bad or embarrassing yourself, I'm willing to bet that failing is never something you planned for. You didn't plan to lose that job. You never wanted to become broke, divorced, or feeling like you're all alone without a friend in the world. You never planned to let the team down, or to make that critical error on the report that cost the company thousands.

I'll bet everything you've ever achieved had a certain level of careful planning to it. And why do we plan everything out? To avoid mistakes and failing in the first place.

But mistakes are inevitable.

I heard someone say once, "The only thing I ever failed at is life." And what is this life but a bucket of trials and errors? But do you know who fails the most?

The people who plunge forward fearlessly are the real failures. It poises them to take the future no matter what, ready to fail fast. Success is only part of the journey, like a goal post they hit on the way, but it is not the destination.

Your aim is to turn failure into your best friend. The fear of failing must become your greatest weapon. This runs against everything they ever taught you in the actual world; In school, at work, and in your own family, where failure is frowned upon and fear is to be avoided, you must be ready to take your fear head on no matter what the odds or outcome.

When you are trained that fear is bad, it controls all your decisions. You maneuver through life, dodging dangerous obstacles (opportunities) and avoid risk at all costs. Learning to play it safe to keep the peace, your heart and mind become restless. You settle for the easy way.

The easy way eventually turns into the hard way, and you recognize that everything you have ever wanted is on the other side of all your fears.

Yes, those same fears that you have been avoiding most of your life.

The fear of failing. The fear of looking stupid. The fear of loss. The fear of what other people will think. The fear of living a life without meaning.

The **fear of living**.

If this sounds like your story, you're in the right place. Together we can figure this out and, before you are halfway through *Fail Big*, you will push forward fearlessly, and failing as you go.

After all, *what do you have to lose?*

Your life will end someday—maybe soon—and when it does, will you leave this world with a heart full of joy, knowing that you did everything you could to master change? Or will you wither away slowly, trapped in a life made up of regret and discontent?

You don't want that, and I don't want that. Your mission is to kill every chance for regret to take over your mind. Regret is the result of doing nothing to make your dreams happen.

In the end, you might fail. That is the risk. But the biggest failure of all is giving up and choosing to do nothing.

What *Fail Big* Means for You

If you want to stop failing, there is a simple solution for that: Find something really boring to do and just repeat the same thing every day for the rest of your life. You can't fail at what is easy. You won't fail when you live inside a zone of comfort.

Do nothing, say nothing, and try nothing is how you stop yourself from failing. But you still live scared. The fear of failing is your master.

You want more from this life than it is ready to give you, and you have the courage to reach up and take it. But this journey will not be easy. There will be challenges that push you back. It will upset people with the new you and some might leave because they fear what you're becoming. I say let them go. Let it all go if it means that you are pushing forward and doing what you have always dreamed of doing, even if it scares the hell out of you.

But the question many ask is, *"How can I fail forward, and be a success at the same time?"*

It isn't failing that makes you a success. It is your perception of it. Many people fail in life and beat themselves up when nothing goes right. They become too scared to try again. They develop a victim persona that fuels the fear of failure.

You think, *"What if the next time is the BIG ONE where I lose it all? I better play it safe and not take that risk again."*

So, we settle and fall into a life of mediocre comfort. You will never achieve greatness on any level if you accept your situation as hopeless, or you have decided that you've gone as far as you are going to go.

Another question I get asked is, *"What if I fail so many times that it becomes the only thing I'm good at? Won't I see myself as a failure?"*

If Abraham Lincoln was alive right now, what would he say to that? How about Thomas Edison? This is the point you need to question: *Will I be defeated by failure, or motivated because of it? Will it ruin me, or push me forward with relentless ambition?*

As you're reading this book, I want you to ask yourself:

- *What does Failing really mean to me?*
- *What decision have I been putting off?*
- *What action am I avoiding?*
- *Am I on the path that I have always wanted to take, or still living scared and waiting for life to change?*

There are no right or wrong answers here. This is not a test you can fail. You are not in school anymore, and nobody is telling you what to do or how to do it.

You have the key to destiny in your own hands.

Throughout this book, we will look at the strategies and tips for learning to *Fail Big*. But when you conquer your internal fear of failure, it is an absolutely rewarding feeling.

It diminishes all those negative emotions and feelings of unworthiness. You can recognize when you are escaping. You start to feel good about yourself and that feeling of shame is less. Work for it, and recovery will take time. But start today.

Failing is not the fearful beast we have made it out to be. As you'll see throughout the rest of this book, failing is your companion on this journey.

Scott Allan

The *Secret* to Success

"Never, never, never give up."

— Winston Churchill

I had a mentor who once claimed to have the ultimate secret to success. In fact, his claims were so profound that he had hundreds of people asking to be mentored by him, even though he charged $500 an hour. And yet, while he could have taken all their money and made an easy fortune, he turned most of them down. Of the many who wanted to hire him, my mentor only ever worked with two people.

When someone asked him why he was so selective in his hiring process, he said:

"Most people aren't ready for what they have to do to succeed. They want a mentor because they think there is a special formula or trade secret I will give them they can't get anywhere else. And they are so desperate for it, most will pay anything to avoid the pitfalls along the way. That's not what I teach. I instruct people on what to do when (not IF) they fail and what to do about it. But most aren't ready for failing. My first lesson is always, "Learn to fail". Most give up after that."

Learning to Fail

But just as money can't buy you love, it also can't buy you success. If having money meant happiness, I wouldn't have so many rich clients. Most of them had cash and weren't afraid to use it. But the problem was deeper than money stability. Most were afraid they would die… afraid. They could buy anything they wanted, yes, but many couldn't buy the one thing they craved the most: the courage to be themselves, to live life as free souls capable of living fearlessly.

When I shared my secret with the clients who were ready for it, they too learned to live as fearless warriors. We all want to be that fearless warrior. The person who can go up against anything and win. Many of us want to be the hero in our own story, but when we really take that inward look into who we "think" we are, the empire crumbles. Most people have a weak, distorted view of themselves that is wired in fantasy.

We want to live a fearless lifestyle. To be the master of your destiny is the ultimate dream, but when it comes time to face those actual fears of failure, criticism, and rejection, it all comes apart. Failing—if you haven't done enough of it—becomes the outcome you would do anything to avoid.

How do you avoid failing at anything? Simple: you avoid doing it. This is a hard fact: most people fail without taking any action at all. They fail by not showing up for the big game, so they fail by default. This form of self-sabotage is difficult to detect.

When you're on the playing field of life and you lose the big game, you're on stage for everyone to see. Your failing is public record. But this is where growth begins.

You learn by doing. Everything that you succeed at is a measure of risk taken. If you gamble everything you have, you risk losing it all. If you win, you take home the earnings. We are afraid of losing that hand, so we hold on to it. But life is impatient. It waits for nobody. You are here to play the game or watch the game. The risk-takers are on the field, win or lose, and usually both.

This is where *Fail Big* comes in. This book is about the journey of that fearless warrior. When you believe in the big WHY of your mission, it removes ME from the equation. It is not about you any more than it is about me. Believe it or don't believe it, you are capable of greatness, even if you are not at a place in your life where it feels that way.

You could lack confidence (who isn't, right?) and self-esteem issues (been there before, right?) are holding you back from plunging ahead and, as Nike would say, "Just Do It."

Do it now. Start today. Go out into the world scared and embrace your fears.

Fail Big is not just another book that makes you feel good and pumps you up with motivational tactics that never see the light of day. I will introduce you to dozens of entrepreneurs and creatives that embraced failure as the golden ticket to success and plunged forward, many losing everything, to come back stronger than ever.

In *Fail Big*, you will learn how to:

- Master the psychological influence of failure

- Embrace the fear of taking risks

- Reduce your failure rate by developing your skills

- Disengage your failure mindset

- Deal with failure even when it isn't yours.

Developing a *Fail Big* Action Plan

Now, before we dive into the first chapter, consider this question:

What is your attitude towards failure? Do you have a positive or negative perception of failure? How do you deal with problems when they occur? Do you avoid obstacles instead of tackling them head-on?

No matter the failures you've had in the past, I want you to grasp these moments in your life as much-needed learning curves that have a higher purpose. It didn't seem like it then, and if you are struggling today, it might not seem like it now, but the action you take and the difference you make will measure your achievements in this lifetime.

I spent my life afraid of failing and making mistakes, looking stupid, covering up when I messed up, and then lying to cover up the mess. I learned many lessons about how to handle fear and the importance of letting people see you for who you really are. I knew that getting over the blame and shame would open new pathways that I had never experienced before. In this book, I'll dive into that more.

Why am I telling you this? Because I believe you are here for a big reason. It is this reason that brought us together in this book.

Successful Living *Is* the Journey

This is an incredible journey you are taking. To live a purpose-driven life is a magnificent feat. Many people, when they set out to succeed towards a goal, become so immersed in reaching the destination that they forget—the struggle to get there is the goal. It's the hard work you put in, the sacrifice you make to work on your dream, and the skills and tactics learned to prepare yourself for success.

But getting there is only the beginning. Your life will become a chain of successes as you learn to conquer new obstacles, take on tough challenges without fear of failing, and making a commitment to push hard when something or someone pushes hard against you.

To *Fail Big* is about all the steps you take from here to there, often not knowing if each step is the right one to take, then eventually not caring if it is. Taking that step—stepping into action—is what winners do.

How many people do you know that have given up their dreams because they stopped moving forward? Why did they give up? They stopped taking those critical steps. Fear gets in the way and it has a powerful voice. It says, "If you can't do it right, don't do it at all" or, "The time to succeed was ten years ago, and now it's too late."

It is never too late, unless you believe it is. As long as you have air in your lungs and an ounce of ambition left, you can grow that single seed into something unstoppable. You can *Fail Big* when most are just failing by default.

My favorite quote on failure is by mega-bestselling author, J. K. Rowling: *"It is impossible to live without failing at something, unless you live so cautiously that you might as well not have lived at all—in which case, you fail by default."*— **J.K. Rowling**

It's better to fail doing what you love to do. You can only push forward when you fail forward. Inaction leads to failing by default when you dream about the life you could have had because you didn't take intentional action when you had the chance.

Fail Big: Your Greatest Reward

Throughout this book, we will look at the strategies and tips for learning to fail big. But when you conquer your internal fear of failure, it is an absolutely rewarding feeling. It diminishes all those negative emotions and feelings of unworthiness. You can recognize when you are escaping and you start feeling good about yourself.

You will have to work for it, and recovery will take time. But start today. The sooner you start, the sooner you'll begin to feel good about yourself. Failing is not the fearful beast we have made it out to be. As you'll see throughout the rest of this book, failing is your companion on this journey.

A friend of mine who was the top salesperson in his organization had a saying that he would make all the salespeople repeat before they went out to sell for the day:

"No fail, so sale."

You will learn to appreciate the act of practicing failing while making leaps and bounds towards success.

Are you ready to *Fail Big* and achieve the impossible?

It's time to take that first step…

'Hard-working' is what gets the job done. You just see that year after year. The students who thrive are not necessarily the ones who come in with the perfect scores. It's the ones who love what they're doing and go at it vigorously.

— **Dr. Carol S. Dweck,** bestselling author of *Mindset: Changing the Way You Think to Fulfill Your Potential*

The Psychological Influence of Failure

We all respond to failure differently. Some people can handle it well and push through the painful experience. Others freeze up, lose total confidence, and feel so demotivated and helpless that they never risk failing again.

How you deal with your own failure is critical to your overall level of happiness and personal satisfaction.

As I'll show you, the *psychological impact of failure* has a powerful influence on the way you live out your life. It influences the work you do, the people you hang out with, the decisions you make (or don't make), the opportunities you attract (or don't attract), and the quality of life experiences that you have.

Failure influences us in two ways:

1. **Failure is a great learning curve.** It's an educational experience, and you can implement your failings to do better the next time. Just as the salesperson keeps trying over and over to get that sale after hundreds of rejections, you turn failure into an ally, figure out an alternative approach, and pursue your goals relentlessly.

2. **Failing scares you**. At the very least, you are intimidated by the thought of failing. You play it safe and take small chances, too small to have any significant impact.

Failure makes you question your self-worth, level of skill, and shakes your confidence so much that it could take you months to recover after one incident. Failure brings about stress and leverages fear so badly that you become depressed and feel totally worthless, helpless, and ashamed.

Failure Avoidance

It's not a surprise we are afraid to fail. The psychological trauma can have a lifelong impact. This causes us to stay away from the ledge for fear of falling off. It induces failure avoidance, which is when we are so fearful of making a mistake and screwing up that we do absolutely anything to avoid failing.

But...avoiding failure doesn't mean you get off the hook. In fact, it has the opposite effect. By living life so carefully, you end up avoiding the great opportunities that come your way.

As JK Rowling has said, *"If you live your life with such caution, trying to avoid failing at all costs, you end up failing by default for not taking action. Either way, you lose."*

Failure. Disruptions. Unexpected events. These do and will happen. The question is, are you psychologically prepared for it? Do you have a plan for when good turns bad? It's okay if you don't. Most people are unprepared because we are trained to deal with the crisis when it happens. But by that time, it's too late. You don't suddenly develop the right mindset or skills to handle failure when it occurs.

The psychology of handling failure starts with preparing for battle before the war begins. You can't expect to win the fight if you wait until the night before to begin training. The other guys have been training for months and are fully prepared. Lack of preparation and false expectations leads to failure by default. You fail before the fight, and not during it.

This is what it's like to deal with life's failings. If you attempt to avoid failing, it's the same as just giving up. This is self-sabotage. Mentally, we know failure is inevitable, but knowing it and accepting it as a reality are two different things.

It is breaking apart the "better you than me" syndrome. If you've ever witnessed a friend going through a nasty divorce or financial trouble, you may have caught yourself saying, "Better him than me." This is as if to say you're off the hook and these things won't happen to you. Psychologically, you're thinking you escaped having to go through such an experience.

But just wait... everyone has their day. Today, it is your best friend, but it could be you next week. Does this thought scare you?

Be ready to embrace the worst, and you will develop immense gratitude for the best of days. You can't avoid failing any more than you can avoid dying. The best you can do is prepare for it so you're equipped and ready when the day arrives.

The Persuasive Power of Failing

Failure is very persuasive. It affects your happiness, self-esteem, and confidence. One enormous loss could set you back for months, years or decades. You might say, "I'd rather never face that trial again, so I'm playing it safe from now on." The psychological impact of failing causes us to retreat to safer ground.

"Successful people don't fear failure but understand that it's necessary to learn and grow from.

— Robert Kiyosaki

Safety is a comfort zone that has its own dangers. You become weak when you close the door on future opportunities and rely on the stability of routine.

A friend of mine—Tony—had several job offers in the same year that paid more with better working conditions. He wanted to take one of these jobs, but in the end, he turned them all down. Why? His current job was steady, didn't challenge him much, and even though he was bored in the current position, switching to another company he didn't know was risky. What if it didn't work out? What if they didn't like him?

He stayed with the stable choice, and six months later, the job let him go. Downsizing. He contacted a company that had offered him a job six months prior, but they had filled that position and were no longer hiring. Tony admitted that the fear of failing in the new role held him back. To avoid this, he took the easy path—do nothing and stick with what is working.

This is a form of self-sabotage.

We do this every day, making choices based on the risk factor involved, but our focus is on the losses that could be incurred instead of the gains. To use gambling as an example, you might lose $100 if you play the game. But you could stand to win 10x that if you succeed. Taking a risk is always a gamble. If you play a safe hand and you can still lose.

Failure Expectation and Sabotage

Sabotaging your chances of success is easy because it takes the pressure off. You've already decided beforehand that you're going to fail at your own accord. Nobody has power over you. I remember showing up for tests in school knowing I hadn't studied for a single minute and, not only was I planning my failure ahead of time, but it saved me from having to wait for the outcome: did I pass or not? Am I a failure or a winner? Will they hold me back or let me move ahead? What if they find out what a failure I really am?

When your mind is riddled with self-doubt, the fear of a bad outcome, or failure expectation, it removes the risk of being disappointed. By setting up your failure ahead of time, you are in control of the outcome. You know you're going to fail, but at least you have nobody to blame but yourself.

This is a psychological twist. It took me years to recognize how I was setting up my failings ahead of the game. I figured, if everyone is expecting me to lose, why disappoint them? Better yet, why give them the satisfaction of failing me? I'll do it myself and then they can't claim victory. This is how I used to operate because I was drowning in hopelessness and thrived on failing as the only outcome I could control.

I learned to fail early in life, but my "failure education" was twisted. I learned to fear the risk of taking chances. When your self-esteem is low, you have little confidence in your decision-making power. You not only feel like a failure, but at your core, you become one. It's a devastating way to live, but many do live this way. People deal with it through escape, evasion, or blending into the shadows, hoping to go unnoticed.

To fail is to learn. When you learn, you step up your game. If you're not learning and making mistakes, you could be living scared.

Don't make "failure by default" your only strategy.

The Psychological Impact of Failure

Failing influences your life in many ways. Depending on the culture and environment you grow up in, the results can be devastatingly hard. You might try to please your parents, teachers, peers, your manager, or an institution that is deciding to hire you. Your life could hang in the balance if the person on the other end of the table is making a decision that could impact your future.

The fear is real and failing is real. But it is the courage you reveal by showing up to play the game that matters. For many years, I ran away from failure. And if I wasn't running from it, I was trying to create chaos that made my life fail with intention.

This is what happens when your confidence, self-esteem and purpose are out of alignment. You feel so down about yourself that your attitude says, "Whatever happens, happens. Just get it over with."

This form of negativity influences the circumstances to turn against you. It breeds more failure and keeps the fear real.

We all approach failing from either a negative or positive perspective. If I fail at something, it wasn't meant to be. If I succeed, I did something right. But win or lose, it doesn't matter. Stepping up to bat, knowing that the pitcher is one of the best in the world and your chances of striking out are 9/10, no matter the outcome, you showed up to play.

Striking out in life is like this. Going the distance is about finishing the race, and not coming in first. If winning is all there was, then in a marathon with 500 runners, that means 499 are failures, right? I don't think so.

I ran my first marathon three years ago. I remember when I started thinking about how badly I wanted to get there first. I tried getting ahead of everybody I could, but less than halfway, I could barely run anymore. People twice my age were passing me. I stopped to rest for a while, and the rest of the race was a gentle stride to the finish.

When I got to the end of that line, I was expecting people to be pointing, saying things like, "Look at this guy, he barely made it." But instead, I was given a small reward for finishing. People were patting me on the back, saying, "You made it!" My perspective changed that day. What I had viewed as a humiliation was really a victory. Later, it occurred to me that most of my life had been spent this way, believing that he who finishes second place has lost the race.

Failure is not the negative event we have made it out to be. It is just the reverse. Failure is your best friend, and the positive power it has is truly amazing. Failure will never lie or betray you. It is only deceptive when you try to pretend it doesn't exist. The hard way is the only way for high-performance champions.

We try to avoid making mistakes in order to dodge the bullet, but as you may have seen already, the only thing you're dodging is your road to freedom. Failure provides opportunity in a way that nothing else can. A good friend of mine, who is successful in business and in life, once said: *"I'm here now because of the failures I made along the way."*

Do you realize that the #1 reason people don't have what they want in life isn't because they failed to get it? This is how it may seem, but the real reason is that they didn't fail enough. They didn't take enough risks. They didn't love enough. They didn't act when they should have. They didn't move in the moment but remained frozen in fear until the moment passed.

Failure is your optimum growth tool. It is your weapon in the big game. It is not just the road to success, but it *is* the road you must be willing to take because most people refuse to do so. It is the *Road Less Traveled* that has the best sights on the way.

> *"Two roads diverged in a wood and I - I took the one less traveled by, and that has made all the difference."*
>
> ## — Robert Frost

If you are looking for an easy way to live, you won't find it here. I know lots of people who are always trying to find that easy path to get ahead. Guess what? They are all struggling because they keep starting over. They get stuck and give up or go back to the beginning again.

The act of failure has a great influence on your life. Where you are today is in direct relation to the struggle you went through to get here. The struggle from here (where you are now) to there (where you desire to be) is the journey.

The choices you make today will influence the journey you commit to undertake. This is why you must be self-aware of where you are in the moment. Who are you spending time with? How are you spending your time? What are you doing with your time? How much time do you have today to work on your one thing that really matters?

What makes you different from that person who is succeeding? Is he or she luckier? Born privileged? Has an upper hand? You might make yourself believe that successful people have it better off or that they had help, someone gave them a lucky break that you'll never get, or they just happened to be in the right spot at the right time.

Believe what you want but, all those thoughts set us up to fail. We fail the minute we convince ourselves that it isn't possible. You start to think, "I can't have this thing I truly want, so I'll settle for what life gives me."

If you settle for what you can get, you will always get what you ask for, which is usually what you never wanted in the first place. The first rule is to stop wishing for things that you truly must have and build a plan to go after it.

There are always so many excuses for why something can't be done. Here is a short list:

- "But you see, I tried that. It didn't work."

- "Someone said that…"

- "It seems like a lot of work."

- "What if it doesn't work out the way I want?"

- "I heard that it is risky."

- "If you keep failing, you will never be successful."

- "If I fail, it must mean I'm a failure!"

- "My peers always said that I would amount to nothing. Maybe they were right?"

You fail yourself the second you start to verbally project your defeat before it happens. Most people never get the chance to find out what it is like to fail because they're too busy avoiding it.

Put yourself in Abraham Lincoln's shoes. What would it have been like for a man surrounded by death, strife, people wanting him to fail, trying to make him fail, and along the way, losing loved ones, friends and family? Did he give up?

No, but he could have.

Many would have been happy if he had because the changes he dictated took away from the rich and made the poor free. Would he have done all this if he had known that he'd be killed by a lone assassin? If he had not, if he had lost and taken his losses to the grave without pushing forward, history would have been written differently.

Lincoln created his own history book. No matter how we try to frame or reframe it, he made decisions based on values that he knew to be right. He was a man of hard-core principles and always carried his mission forward without fear of scrutiny. Lincoln persevered, showed tough grit, and succeeded to accomplish his goals no matter the challenges he faced.

In the end, his losses mattered none. His failures mattered none. What people said about him or did to him mattered none. Through all of that, he could march ahead towards that goal of becoming president and then, with the leverage of power in his hands, made history happen.

Here is my question to you: what is your history going to look like? What will you do, how will you respond when defeat is staring you down, and all you have at your disposal is the willpower to carry on? What are you prepared to do when the odds are stacked so high against you it would be impossible to leap? But what is impossible but a state of mind?

Taking a risk, such as deciding to fly around the world in nothing but a small plane, sounds crazy. Who would do that, and why? It is a machine, and machines break down. But this didn't prevent Amelia Earhart from becoming the first female pilot to fly solo across the Atlantic Ocean. Had she calculated her chances of success, she may have realized her chances of failing were high. In the end, her plane was lost at sea and they never found her.

Did she fail successfully? You can draw your own conclusion. But, if she hadn't taken the risks she had, her story of courage and perseverance would never have existed. Perhaps Amelia would have lived to be a very old age and had a different life. How do you compare a life long-lived to a life well-lived?

Many people throughout history have died doing what they love, driven by a purpose many could never understand, but relentless in their pursuits, pushing on towards the end even if it meant certain death.

How far are you willing to go to pursue your ultimate purpose? At what stage would you consider giving up? What price are you willing to pay to discover the impossibilities of success that wait for you?

Disengage Your Failure Mindset

"Winners are not afraid of losing. But losers are. Failure is part of the process of success. People who avoid failure also avoid success."

— **Robert T. Kiyosaki**, Author of
Rich Dad, Poor Dad

Failing in life is an inevitable outcome. Try to think back to a time in your life when you succeeded at everything. You've failed at tests, sports, relationships, and work. In some ways, you have failed yourself by not living up to your maximum potential. In every aspect of your life, making critical mistakes—and what you label as a "failure"—actually is progress.

Some people see failure as something to be feared and avoided. They stay away from pushing beyond their limits because failing is a demoralizing, emotionally painful experience and reduces self-esteem.

There are others who see failing as a necessary step to getting where they need to go. On the other side of failure is everything you've ever wanted and more. But when you fear failure to the extent it paralyzes your mind, your life becomes trapped in a bubble, unable to break free.

Get Unstuck from Your Failure Mindset

Failing can induce stress and make us question our worth and competency. We experience deep fears driven by anxiety. Failure—and the fear it creates—is persuasive and manipulative. We become convinced that we have no chance, so we leave all risks on the table and opt for the simple way out. But the easy way is the path to losing everything you could be gaining.

Are you ready to give up, walk away and let failure rob you of all you could have if you were willing to take risks? I didn't think so.

Now, take a minute to consider these questions:

- Do you minimize your achievements and believe your success isn't justified?

- Do you think that you haven't accomplished as much as others, and that you need to prove yourself even further?

- Are you attached to the failures of your past, and do you believe they'll be your future?

- Are you avoiding any form of responsibility because you want to avoid failing?

Trapped by Failure

People who struggle with a failure mindset have been subjected to:

- Harsh criticism

- Rejection issues

- Perfectionistic ideals

- Unrealistic expectations

- Humiliating moments

- Lack of belief in themselves and from others

- Lack of love (from childhood and personal relationships)

When we are made to believe we are worthless, it creates deeper feelings of defectiveness. We then carry this feeling of defectiveness into every aspect of our lives. We develop a self-defeating mindset that we are never good enough no matter what we do, and that failing is an expectation we learn to live with.

For example, we choose relationships with people who end up controlling or mistreating us. You might take on a role in your job because it places you in a position of power over others. You try nothing new because you expect to fail before you even do anything. Just the thought of facing your fear of failure creates anxiety and social exclusion.

The obvious failures we have all experienced can be observed by everyone: a bad report card in school, losing a client in your business, or a failed relationship, such as a bad breakup or marriage. But the failure nobody can see is the only one you know about: the failure of self. It is the most painful failure of all because it is internal.

When we fail, it validates all the feelings we have that we are no good. But nobody is born a failure. It happens from years of negative conditioning. We are trained to fear failure and, therefore, conditioned to fear change. By resisting failing in life, you are choosing to escape. Our avoidance strategies keep us stuck in a perpetual loop of self-defeat.

Before we go any further, I want you to make a failure list. Write all the things you feel you have failed at, such as relationships, jobs, or anything else you can think of.

Here is my short list:

1. Failed to get into university after high school

2. Failed twice at starting my business

3. Failed my driving test three times

4. Failed to be my best in relationships

I failed at a lot of things, but I succeeded at many as well. Through making mistakes, I learned about everything that doesn't work. This is how we can close the gap on our errors and move closer to success.

Next, make a list of ten things you have succeeded at that you are happy with. You can follow up on how your failures in life later turned into successes. For example, I failed at business several times, but I eventually succeeded as well because I stayed with it. I failed courses in school like many people, but it only made me more determined to succeed. Eventually, I would go on to college and graduate.

Failure does not have to be a permanent condition, as we will see. You might fail today at what you are striving for, but eventually, if you stick and keep working at it with a driven passion, you'll look back someday with gratitude for the lesson the struggle taught you.

If you are ready, let's look at the fear of failure, what it does, where it comes from and the strategies we can implement and put into action for recovery.

The Anatomy of a Failure Mindset

My father was a very successful man. He excelled in business and was a leader in his industry for many years. The companies he worked for throughout his 35-year career paid him well, and he was flown all over the country to attend conferences and deliver speeches.

But he had one fatal flaw that nobody knew about: he believed he was worthless at his core, a failure, and constantly came up short when he compared himself to his competition.

From the outside, he appeared to be highly successful with a secure job, credentials, a big house, and a yacht. But it wasn't enough. He struggled to accept himself as he was, striving instead to become someone he respected and admired. The battle he fought wasn't with his competitors in business. It was with himself.

One night, he told me this story. "There I was in this boardroom with these other business people. Some of them were billionaires and men with empires. They would look at me and ask me for my opinion on how they should close a deal or beat their competition. Whenever this happened, all I could think about was, 'What are you asking me for? I only have a grade 11 education!'"

My father never finished high school, and he carried it with him throughout his entire life. His parents thought he should quit and get a 'real job'. Because of a lack of support at home with parents who cared little for his future, he stopped going to school. But he was a smart man and wanted to succeed.

He worked hard to get to an executive level in his industry, but the feeling of failure always stuck. He never deemed himself worthy to be in a room with a bunch of other people who had degrees, billions of dollars, and lived in houses larger than most small towns. He spent much of his life trapped with a fear of failing because he listened to his negative voices feeding him false messages.

The voices from our past, and the negative actions that were done to us, largely shape the level of success we experience. It is an enigma of how someone who achieves more than the average person can still deem themselves unworthy, no matter what they've got.

> *"It's only when you risk failure that you discover things. When you play it safe, you're not expressing the utmost of your human experience."*
>
> **— Lupita Nyong'o**

You might be successful, but until you accept that you're good enough and everything you have is a gift that requires gratitude, you will always be poor. I have met many people in life who had it all externally, but internally, they were completely bankrupt and could never enjoy what they had.

Not only do we fear failing, but we live it. We walk around with the belief that we're not good enough. We work hard, play hard, and take life seriously so as not to let our guard down. We have this ongoing feeling of shame, as if it embarrasses us to be ourselves and would rather be someone else.

Just like the social level of self-defeat, we don't deem ourselves worthy of having, being or owning anything. We enter relationships with dependence issues, and we carry around a heavy burden. We feel incomplete.

"If only I can prove myself with one more success, more money, or a higher social status."

This is a perpetual self-defeating cycle that never stops. Not until we put an end to it through creating a stream of thinking that lifts up our negativity.

It has nothing to do with success. You don't get over failure by succeeding and racking up achievements.

If you struggle with the failure mindset, you might have a few or all of these characteristics. This isn't a quiz; use this to identify the core traits you use most often:

You are deeply entrenched in a failure mindset if you:

- Pursue success relentlessly but you're never satisfied.

- Can never measure up to the people you compare yourself to.

- Minimize your skills, abilities, and capacity for success.

- Feel like a phony and believe others will find you out eventually.

- Set yourself up for failure because, if you succeed, you'll be given more responsibility that you're sure you'll fail at.

- Believe the worst about yourself, and that every new challenge presented is another chance for you to screw up.

- Obsess about what others think of you, causing you to exaggerate and make things up.

- Do as little as possible to avoid standing out.

- Are afraid of making commitments.

- Have an expectation of failure, so you sabotage your chances of succeeding before you even try.

External Appearance vs. Internal Convictions

If you are trapped in a failure mindset, you are in a lot of internal pain that nobody can see or feel but you. You know it is there because you feel it every day, like a secret you keep close to the surface but just deep enough that it stays hidden.

Nobody knows your fear like you do. So, to keep this secret buried, you avoid taking risks. Your failure mindset holds you back, and you're paralyzed to move ahead or draw attention to yourself. You're terrified that you might be asked to take on greater responsibility, and risk feeling shame. You'd rather operate from behind the fragile walls of your ego and fear-based mindset.

The Critics and People Who Are Wrong

With failure, we are our own worst critics. The world doesn't have to do anything to contribute to our feelings of inferiority. We can do enough of that ourselves. On the surface, we can appear confident, in control, and make big decisions.

But the actual battle is the internal struggle we cope with day-to-day. It is facing that inner sense of failure. You might appear to have it together, but inwardly, you are terrified of being exposed as the fraud you believe you are.

Struggling to cope with your inner feelings of perfection, shame and failure, it diminishes your ability to believe in yourself. You think that no matter what you do, it'll never be good enough.

Perhaps you had a similar experience as a child which caused this belief. The feeling of not being able to measure up, that you might disappoint someone—usually your parents—or your tendency to destroy your chances of success through self-sabotage.

Why would we sabotage ourselves? There are several reasons. First, if you set yourself up to fail, nobody will expect anything from you. You'll be left alone, which is what most people who struggle with their negative emotions long for. We want the world to act as if we don't exist. This way, nobody is watching. You can live your life in peace with your negative vices and nobody will criticize you.

By self-sabotaging, the pressure is off and now we can validate all of our excuses for not trying anything. "You see, I told you it was too difficult," or how about, "That's the last time I try that." But sabotage is a method for escape. It is a survival mechanism we have developed to avoid the pain of facing failure.

The self-sabotage strategy is like a silent enemy. We don't know it's there until we look for it. If you have a pattern or history of failing at something, chances are you already know this subconsciously. Now is your chance to bring it to the surface and expose it for what it is. You can only stop destructive behavior when you see the power it has and how it is manipulating your actions.

As children, we were often:

- Criticized

- Pushed to succeed and berated when we didn't

- Expected to meet certain criteria before we were given love

- Scrutinized for trying to be unique.

Escape Methods

We now know that we use avoidance tactics to sabotage ourselves so we don't have to be responsible for our successes or failures.

But the road seems impossible to navigate when there are obstacles at every corner. And if you are like me, you've been maneuvering around difficult obstacles most of your life. It is exhausting. Throughout our lives, escape has become a default action when we want to avoid failing. Relationships, work or personal issues are abandoned. We do not deal problems with, but push them aside.

There are several tactics we used to practice avoiding what we don't want to deal with. You might procrastinate and put things off indefinitely or distract yourself with other tasks to avoid the things that demand your attention. Escape is a means of sabotage. You can run, but you'll never recover. We can only get better if we take a stand and choose to not be defeated.

Years ago, when I first noticed my methods of escape, I could see the patterns I was practicing almost daily. I would avoid talking about difficult subjects such as relationship problems. My attitude was, "It will work itself out." But then it was handled by someone else, or it was not taken care of at all.

Problem avoidance is an escape from reality. It is a tactic for survival. Because we never learned to deal with our reality as children, we have developed our own methods of coping. It may not be healthy, but it creates a feeling of inner security. We learned to survive because we had no choice.

When the world makes you feel you are no good, you seek to escape from it.

Procrastination and Minimizing

Similar to problem avoidance, procrastination is a powerful self-defeating habit that can develop from childhood. It holds us back from taking immediate action and ruins our chances for succeeding at anything worthy.

To avoid failing, procrastination is the number one choice for many. It is self-sabotage on many levels. It is a vicious cycle of self-defeat. Of course, many people procrastinate to varying degrees, but some of us have turned it into a habit of survival.

When it is the first default factor that we turn to for escape, it puts everything on hold. You cannot recover when you are busy burying the pain. The opposite of procrastination is taking massive action. These are the action steps that move you out of your pain.

Brushing off praise is another method of avoidance, but with this tactic, you are minimizing your achievement because you believe it is worthless. You think anybody could have done it, so it wasn't a big deal. You'll just try harder the next time to do a better job.

By minimizing your own success, you never actually crawl out of the self-pity failure rut. You continue to go for the next big win, but it doesn't last long.

The Failure Mindset Relaunch

Now that we have looked at this mindset, let's get into the strategies we can use to relaunch your action plan. I am going to lay out four strategies you can put into action to recover from and mend your failure mindset.

I suggest you focus on just one strategy at a time. Don't overwhelm yourself and think you have to heal in a week. You cannot rush progress.

1. Talk back to the negative mindset

There are people in our past who wronged us. They treated us unfairly, criticized our mistakes, and made us feel as if we were major disappointments.

When we return to this point in our past, it brings up painful memories. But we need to examine it because we tried to avoid the reality of what happened. The things we ignore eat away at us over time. This leads to depression, anger, and deep pain that never have time to heal. We can heal this now.

Confront the people you're angry with. Imagine what it would be like to visit this person and tell them how you feel. What are you going to say? This exercise will free you of your shame. Stay firm and don't think for a minute that you deserved to be punished or treated the way you were. If that person were standing in front of you right now, how would you react? What would you say? What would you hold back on?

The fact is, we can't always confront the people that we're still angry or bitter towards. In many cases, we can't do that anyway, or in cases where abuse happened or there's deep emotional scarring, it might be better to stay your distance. But an exercise that works is to imagine this person is with you and you have five minutes to tell them how you feel. Visualize the conversation and how you are able to express your feelings.

You'll find that you can strengthen your ability to forgive. But this isn't necessarily for the other person to feel better. It is for you. By being able to let go of the pain of what happened, you are freeing yourself up for some serious growth.

As long as we stay resentful, angry and bitter, it becomes nearly impossible to move on. You owe it to yourself to level up and step up.

2. Decide to do something you've been putting off

What is it you have been avoiding? Now is your chance to make it work. Your decision will shape all of your days to come from now on. What are you deciding to do? Is it a dream that you once abandoned? Or do you want to reach out to someone you haven't spoken to in a long time?

Recognizing what you are running from is the first step to taking action. Your decisions are powerful. The life you are leading right now has been a direct result of the decisions you made. The direction of a person's life is decided by the choices made in each and every moment.

Indecision creates worry and fear. But decisions made with intention will create the circumstances of your life, today and thirty years from now.

3. Fail forward. Fail often

When we fail at something, the first instinct is to pull back, reassess, and then maybe try again. But many people don't try again. They reassess and then try something less risky, taking another predictable path that will guarantee success. You will not fail this way, but you won't succeed either.

The only way forward is to embrace the lessons you learned and go with it. In fact, the people who fail the most, get the most. They get ahead, and they get what they have always wanted. The rest are fighting for the same scraps because they have one thing in common: they are afraid to take massive action and fail forward. Your defeat is a stepping stone. You can only step up when you've taken three steps back.

4. Make a checklist of how you are going to succeed

This is a powerful task. We know all the ways we have failed. Failure has become our master craft. But what if we carved out a checklist of all the ways we can succeed? For example, here is my short checklist of what I am putting into action for better success:

- Wake up early and exercise.

- Read for thirty minutes a day.

- Take walks more frequently.

- Outline the novel I have always wanted to write.

- Enroll in a course.

- Write a letter to someone who once hurt me, detailing how I forgive him or her. Sending this letter is optional.

- Add up what I'm grateful for at the end of each day. The goal is to hit 20 per day.

- Focus on one goal I have always wanted to achieve.

- List my achievements in the last ten years, no matter how small.

The Fearless Growth Mindset

The success of this *Fail Big* journey begins with your mindset. Mindset is at the center of your universe as you move through this life. If your mind is dialed in wrong, it influences your thoughts, decisions, emotions, and actions.

For every high-performance guru, world-class entrepreneur, business leader, single parent, writer, musical creative, and people from all walks of life, mindset plays a critical role in your success or failure. Beyond talent, skill, money, or social contacts, your own mind—and the relationship you have connected to failure—is responsible for the result of your ultimate outcome.

Failure—and your perception of failing—has a direct relationship with your mindset. This is your attitude, beliefs, and thoughts towards people, events and life in general that interpret what something means to you.

People who have mastered the mind, and have a high ability to learn anything no matter their situation, age, race or personality type, are tapped into the mindset of learning and winning. They have an open mind—a growth mindset—that is necessary for this level of learning.

The more advanced your growth mindset is, the faster your learning cycle. When your mindset is focused on growing, the mental obstacles are destroyed. You forge the attitude that makes or breaks your attitude towards failing.

There are seven key components needed for mastering your growth mindset, and I will teach you what these are later.

Mindset Makes the Difference

The Bottom line: Mindset delivers impact. If you are harboring the mindset of a person who lives in scarcity, believes in fear over taking forward action, and is full of doubt and mistrust, you're setting your mindset to align with these thoughts. In doing so, you decide the course of your destiny.

How you perceive failure, your interpretation of what it means, and the decisions you make that push you ahead to do it scared anyway will always come back to your mindset surrounding failure.

This is why you need to learn about the influence your mindset has above everything else. If you approach life with the "wrong frame of mind", you're going to make living more difficult than it has to be. Most problems that you and I have are created within our own mindset: Worry, anxiety, fear, scarcity, and attitude.

Working through your life with failure—and failing forward—can be an enjoyable experience. You don't believe this yet, but towards the end of this book, the fear of failing—and your perception of failure—will take a positive upswing.

I know that this sounds contrary to everything you've ever been taught about failing. We are conditioned, from a very young age, to believe that failing is bad and success is good. Losing is bad and winning is good. There is no such thing as #2, only #1.

Think about your journey up to this point, and in context, some of the failures that you have endured over the years that brought you here. Conjure up old memories of big mistakes made and how you pushed through them. If you're reading this, it means you've made it. You're here! You might be thinking, *Failure isn't for me*, or *I've always been afraid of it*. Afraid or not, you are still doing what it takes to survive—and thrive—in life.

It is the people who have given up, stopped learning, turned negative and bitter, are filled with regret and resentment, and are now living without hope who suffer the worst failure imaginable— the failure of living. What is the point of having this gift of life if you are not willing to push yourself to grow?

Your life, as soon as you develop the willingness to fail big and crush your obstacles no matter how big they appear, puts you in the winning driver's seat. You don't have to become number one to win the game—you just show up to play, play hard, and don't give in until the game is over.

YOU decide the rules of how you want to fail big, and then you break those rules.

Take a moment to think where you could be six months from now if failure becomes your best friend instead of your worst enemy. What would you take confident action towards from today? How would you feel in finally understanding all the obstacles blocking you could be removed by developing a positive relationship with failure?

Mindset begins with **attitude**. Your attitude sets the scale for your success in everything. When you align your mindset with attitude, you create an unbreakable mental force. You can put an end to harboring negative feelings built around old beliefs, past hurts, and past failures. A change in attitude is deciding to swing up and out of the old way of doing and behaving.

Your mindset is made of two dimensions: **fixed and growth**. To have a mindset that is open to the challenges of failing fast and forward, you should be working from within your growth mindset. This goes for every area of your life.

Personal Relationships. Who hasn't failed in a relationship or a marriage? A fixed mind in a relationship is a hindrance to making the relationship grow. Relationships are, by nature, constantly changing. If you are struggling to keep it the same way, year after year, eventually it breaks down and you lose the fight.

This is one core reason so many relationships do fail. One or both parties are unwilling to contribute to the growth of the relationship. Fear drives the relationship towards failure.

Business and Career. If you have a fixed mindset in your work, you are comfortable with doing the same tasks in the same way for as long as it takes. If a new way is introduced, you are resistant to changing the old system.

You might even quit your job and find another one that allows you to do the same thing again and again. But you make no progress, your life is stagnant, and your opportunity to take on challenges becomes deep-seated obstacles you can't conquer.

The Big Dream. Do you have a dream for your life? A big goal that you must achieve? If you do, you're one of the elites and you need the right mindset to achieve your dreams.

Dream building requires years of consistent action, persistence, and repetitive failing before it begins to work. You know the stories of famous entrepreneurs, business gurus, musicians, actors, authors, or successful home makers who created online businesses … from their kitchens, garages or college dorms, they built empires that will last generations to come.

They all had one thing in common: The willingness to try, to fail, and to learn. They are willing to do whatever it takes to succeed. When you run towards your dreams, you are doing so with the willingness to embrace failure to get there. People who avoid building their dreams are settling for a life of mediocrity. You are playing within your own boundaries and fear controls your destiny.

Leadership, educators, and mentors: We look to our leaders and mentors to show us what it is we should be learning and paying attention to. If you are a coach or mentor—with a growth mindset—you will train others not just to be followers but to lead others to success.

The idea is you don't want people to be just like you, or to stay beneath you, but to use their own ideas and wisdom to create their own thing. A coach, leader, mentor or teacher is in the business of helping others grow.

The willingness to try, to fail, and to learn. These three things are paramount to your willingness to fail big. But to fail big, you are the poker player showing up at the table with nothing more than the willingness to gamble your cash for the bigger stake. You might be scared, but you are willing to take a chance. Your chance turns into opportunity, and this could become the open door you have been looking for.

I have been talking about mindset, and the growth mindset is the mindset we need to succeed. But how do we make sure we are on the right path? How do you know that your mindset is ready, willing, and able?

Carol Dweck, the author of the million-copy bestselling book _Mindset_, writes:

> _"Mindset change is not about picking up a few pointers here and there. It's about seeing things in a new way. When people – couples, coaches and athletes, managers and workers, parents and children, teachers and students – change to a growth mindset, they change from a judge-and-be-judged framework to a learn-and-help-learn framework. Their commitment is to growth, and growth takes plenty of time, effort, and mutual support to achieve and maintain."_

To break it down, let's take a look at the traits of a fixed mind and a growth mind.

Fixed Mindset

If your mindset has been "fixed", here are the common beliefs and thinking patterns of the fixed mind.

Challenges/Obstacles: Challenge scares me because I fail at everything.

Ability and skill: This is what I trained for. It's all I can do. I don't know anything else, and it's too late to learn.

Personal Qualities: This is who I am. My qualities can't be changed now, it is too late once you become an adult.

Money/finances: I've never had money and never will. My parents were always broke and so I'll always be broke.

Job/career: This is what I was trained for and it's all I can do.

Change/Transformation: I've tried to change before but just ended up back where I was. A nothing, a nobody. I don't like change.

Failure: I tried a few times and couldn't make it work. I guess it was too big of a challenge.

Effort: This is the way I've always done things. Why fix it if it isn't broken?

Criticism: If I am criticized, it's because I am no good at something, and others are happy to point that out to me.

Growth Mindset

If you have a growth mindset, you are ready to learn, take on challenges, and fail fast and forward without your ego getting in the way.

Here are the common beliefs and thinking patterns of the growth mindset:

Challenges/Obstacles: I grow from challenges and it helps me to grow. For every obstacle I overcome, it is a way for my character to level up.

Ability and skill: I can learn any kind of skill and succeed at it. There are no limits to this possibility.

Personal Qualities: I can cultivate and change traits or qualities over time. It might not happen right away, but with effort and diligence, I can make a shift.

Money/finances: Money is in abundance. How much I earn or save depends on how much I want.

Job/career: I can do any kind of work with the right amount of training.

Change/Transformation: Nobody stays the same. Change and growth are a part of the life cycle.

Failure: Every time I fail, I have found a way that doesn't work. I can try something else.

Effort: My amount of effort is equal to the rate of success I get.

Criticism: Feedback is constructive, and I can use it to improve and get better for the next time.

The fixed mindset will struggle with the Fail Big concepts in this book. Now, you might be reading through the fixed and growth mindset traits and find that you are 50/50. Or maybe you just realized that your mindset is very fixed and you have work to do in order to develop a stronger growth mindset. That is okay. Not everyone has a mindset that is perfect. That is why you are here. To grow, to learn, and to thrive with the life you have been gifted with.

Your mindset is the key to building another way of life. To gain access, you only need to believe in the growth that is happening as you fail through your life ... and love every minute of it.

I have dedicated much of my life to growth, only because at one stage in my life, I was terrified of failing. I failed at school, I failed at home, and I failed in relationships. But I was able to overcome all of this with one single thought that, to this day, is the formula for my own mindset. It is my own personal mantra that keeps it real.

My daily mantra is a positive force that awakens my mind to limitless possibility. I encourage you to develop your own mindset mantra, but feel free to use this until you create your own. Recite this every morning and it will become your beacon of positive energy.

"I believe in, trust and have great confidence in my abilities to succeed through learning and speaking with the right people. I know without a doubt I can accomplish the wildest dreams I have ever created. If I am held back by an obstacle, I will find a way through it. If I fall, I will get up and keep going. If I fail, I'll try again. I don't give up. I give myself permission to succeed."

Throughout this book, you'll be introduced to you a system of techniques and pragmatic strategies focused on developing your mindset so that you can reframe failure as a positive force in your life.

You will learn to shift your perspective about what failure is and how it will serve as your strategy for success and not the obstacle blocking you from getting there.

I want you to be prepared and excited to engage in this journey. I believe in you and your ability to do great things with your life.

It begins here...

Developing Your Fearless Growth Mindset

Here are five strategies I use to continuously develop my mindset so that I can learn from my failures and grow as a result of it.

(1). Break your limitations by challenging something new.

A common trap is identifying your current skills and ability as fixed. Here is an example of a fixed mindset expression: "I can't do that." But the truth is you just can't do it now, but you will be able to do it tomorrow or next week. Think of everything you can do now that you couldn't do five or 10 years ago or even last week? It is not about who you were but who you are becoming in taking on a new challenge. You can always learn by doing.

Here are some examples:

Playing music

"I can't do it" can be replaced by "I can't do it yet, but if I practice the piano for one hour a day, I will be able to play something."

Writing a book

"I can't write a book, but if I start writing today, I could be a published author in six months."

Using a computer

I'm not very good with technology. But if I take that course on computer basics, I will be 100% more efficient at my work within three weeks.

Swimming and sports:

"I can't swim 10 meters without sinking. But if I join the swimming club and learn to crawl properly, I will soon be swimming laps like Ian Thorpe."

From now on, I want you to monitor your dialogue and catch yourself when you are saying things like:

"I've never been good at…"

"I can't do…"

Turn it into a momentary setback that ends with a positive note. You could also say, "I used to be someone who couldn't (fill in your challenge), but now I can…"

This strategy and habit are a game changer for shifting into your fail big mindset. It is the formula for developing your growth mindset. You have no limitations except for what you set yourself. By being willing to try and improve your situation, no matter how challenging, you turn a "can't" into a "can do!" These challenges boost confidence but also condition you to fail.

Catch yourself when you're using limiting expressions. There are lots of things you can't do, and many more you'll never be able to do, but if there is a skill or exercise that you've always wanted to learn, do it. Start small and scale up.

(2). Create your "mantra journal" of positive quotes and affirmations.

This is a practice that resulted in huge gains for my fail big mindset. Here is what you do: Invest in a nice journal book. I bought one at Barnes and Noble with a leather jacket. It was about $40 but it became my journal of positive creation. I then filled it with positive quotes, affirmations, and my own personal mantra. I write out my goals in this journal too.

When I come across an inspirational positive quote, I write it in the journal. If I create a mantra that speaks the truth about life, mission or becoming the best, I write it down. This journal has become my personal "bible of positivity."

Here is what you do:

1. **Buy a nice journal.** Make sure it is something you will treasure. Don't do this with a cheap notebook or something that will get tossed into the corner and forgotten. Spend money on a nice journal. Check your local bookstore or Amazon.

2. Commit to writing in your journal for ten minutes a day. You can copy a quote or affirmation. You can fill in a page on your thoughts or an idea you had for a new business. This journal will become your ultimate go-to tool for personal inspiration.

Make a list of your favorite quotes. Read these quotes to yourself in the morning. I add one quote per day to my journal. It has become my source of positive inspiration. You will love the creativity of doing this too.

(3). Make a list of big failure wins. If you want to connect with your fear of failure, you have to recognize that it does exist. Most people who fail blindly, and stumble through life without grasping the lessons failure has to teach, avoid failing by pretending it isn't there. What you avoid has a way of blindsiding you.

An exercise that I recommend is making a list of your recent and past failures. Write them down. Read through the list. You can use the journal exercise I suggested.

Make your failure list and state the outcome of that failure. What happened as a result? What did you learn? What would you have done differently?

Here is an example of how to create change using this simple formula below:

My failure is: I was late for a job interview because I slept in.

Result: I failed to get the job I wanted. They wouldn't even see me.

Lesson learned: Get to bed earlier and have two backup alarms.

Identifying your failures allows you to see your progress. Instead of your internal monologue telling you, "You fail all the time," take a stand and challenge that voice. Yes, you may have failed at lots of things. Great. But you are also learning from this experience and turning it into something good. That is your big win, your "big fail" moment.

Failing is never the end result. We tend to see it as the end of everything, and people walk away from it thinking, *Well, that didn't work, I guess it wasn't meant to be.* Give yourself the chance to turn it around.

Here is a challenge for you. Make a list of your top five failures today. Set aside thirty minutes to do this practice. Then add to it throughout the week. Try for a list of thirty, and then increase this to forty. I have a list of forty-seven failures to date. How many can you come up with?

(4). Own your failure. When you make a mistake, cost your employer money, disappoint your family, or you fail your team, there is only one way to really handle it: Claim your mistake. Make it your own. Now the question is do you own it or do you hide it? I'll be honest, I used to be someone who would run or hide. I didn't want to claim the blame. This strategy never works. You always know it was your fault even if you don't admit it publicly.

We have become good at shifting the blame or hunting down those responsible. But when you own it, you take responsibility. There is no griping, pointing, or trying to get someone to own up to their part. You might only be half to blame, and it doesn't matter. Let the other person worry about their half. When you are involved in a situation that goes wrong, and you had a part to play, you step up and take it.

To fail big, we have to act big.

Think about an incident you were involved in where someone got blamed instead of you. How did that make you feel? Do you still think about it? I know I do. Now, given the same situation today, how would you respond? What action would you take? If you can't answer yet, wait until you get further into the book and we will dive into this more.

(5). Take more risks. Now, by taking risks, I don't mean gambling away your savings hoping to win at blackjack or putting your life—or anyone's life—in danger. I am talking about the risks that we avoid because we are afraid of the failed outcome that could occur.

For example, you are working in a job you hate and is not in alignment with your life's purpose. The risk would be quitting your job and doing what you would love to do. Quitting a full-time job is risky if you have bills to pay, and who doesn't, right?

Consider this. While taking this risk could lead to a big failure, what would it cost for you not to take it? Staying in a line of work that makes you unhappy while your life ends one day at a time? I won't sugarcoat this. Life is short, and shorter for some than others.

Right now, can you identify with a risk you didn't take and later regretted? Is there an action you want to take now but you're afraid it won't turn out in your favor? I can't tell you if taking a chance will bring you the outcome you want. What I can say is if you do nothing, nothing changes.

Nothing is guaranteed. If you are waiting for that safe risk that delivers everything to you without the risk of you losing anything, it probably isn't going to generate a lot of change.

Time is limited and waits for nobody. Stop waiting for that perfect moment. You know what you want. What are you waiting for?

Permission granted. A lot of people act as if they need permission to push forward. You only need that from one person:

You. Your permission has been granted. There is nothing else to wait for.

These five practices can take your fail big mindset to another level. You don't have to try everything at once. If I could make a suggestion, start with the **fail big mindset journal.**

Begin by writing out these ideas to get your creative ideas flowing. Here are a few action steps to get you started:

1. List one action you have been procrastinating on. What is it? Then write down an action step you intend to take in the next five minutes.

2. Is there a mistake you have made recently that you failed to own up to? Be honest, we've all been there. Now, when this situation happens again, what will you do?

I use a quote every day for positive reinforcement. Right now, write down your favorite inspirational quotes. These can be from your favorite authors or someone you know personally who has said something you really like.

Nine Mindset Traits of Successful Failures

"Success is not built on success. It's built on failure. It's built on frustration. Sometimes it's built on catastrophe."

— **Sumner Redstone**

High-level achievers have a gift for charging forward and crushing their fears regardless of how challenging they are. But they're not in possession of any "magic" or special skills that the rest of the population doesn't have access to. What it boils down to are specific character traits successful people have implemented as part of their formula for getting things done.

Your perspective towards failing is everything. It's a frame of mind. By developing the positive traits that *Fail Big* winners use, you stop wasting time searching for shortcuts.

These beliefs—your mindset traits—can become your roadmap to failing forward fast.

Trait #1: Successful Failures Embrace Risk as Part of the Fail Fast Formula

As anyone who has made a grand success of their life will tell you, all the risks taken were worth it. High-level failures, people who know what it means to go the distance, are just as afraid as you and I.

But they do it anyway.

Despite losing what they throw on the table, winners show up to play the game. Your mindset must be ready to accept whatever happens, because you know you can handle it.

Most of us are afraid of risk to some extent. You might hesitate before taking a chance because the fear of losing is over empowering your mind. If I take a chance and fail, will I get to try again? Can my confidence take a loss? Will I disappoint my friends and family of they are counting to me to succeed?

You must see the value in your risk. Instead of imaging a negative outcome, visualize what will happen when you succeed. How will your life be changed? How will other peoples' lives be changed?

Risk is a big part of living. You're at risk as soon as you wake up. But it doesn't stop you from getting out of bed, moving throughout the day, going to work, or driving your car through a busy intersection. This is a risk you've become accustomed to.

Now, try a risk that you have been avoiding but, is a necessary step to achieving your goal.

Trait #2: Successful Failures Perceive Failure as a Lifelong Strategy

I can think of many failures I turned away from. I had to step back and re-evaluate whether I would push forward or not. But failing is not an event and it is not the end of the road. It could be an obstacle or a difficult moment I need to push through. If it were easy, everyone would be doing it.

As Winston Churchill said, "Failure isn't fatal, and success is never final." Think about the people who failed many times on the journey, only to end up succeeding years later. On the other end, how about the companies that succeeded by earning billions a year only to go bankrupt?

So, as we will work on our attitude towards failing, it is not a one-time thing. Failure is never permanent, and neither is success. Taking intentional action and committing to the self-discipline of continuous self-improvement is the only formula that works.

Trait #3: Successful Failures Embrace Rejection as a Necessary Element

Rejection is a dominating force. It impacts everyone's confidence to a certain degree. Don't let it hold you back. Don't fail yourself at your own hand. You can download my book about how to live <u>Rejection Free</u>, and use it as a companion book for *Fail Big*.

Let's look at an example of how rejection works in one of two ways.

Two women both work for a sales company. They are both given a challenge to knock on a hundred doors. The challenge is: Don't stop knocking until you've hit all one hundred.

One of the women starts strong, and she actually has eleven sales out of twenty-five homes. But then his streak wanes and, at the last twenty-five homes, she gets rejected again and again. Feeling like a failure, she eventually quits and goes home.

The other woman hits all one hundred homes. But she doesn't hit a single sale until house #89. She was rejected by 88 customers until she sold her first product. Then, she continued on to the rest of the homes, completing her target of all one-hundred. But, in total, she still only sold one product.

When the president of the company heard about this, he nominated the woman for the employee of the month, not based on the amount of sales but, her commitment for perseverance. In spite of the rejection received, she pushed forward, rejection after rejection, until she got that first win.

When asked how she pushed on with so many people rejecting her sales pitch, she said, "They aren't rejecting me. They are saying no to the product. They don't even see the salesperson. At least, that's how I perceive it."

She also said, "Most sales people take NO personally, but when someone walks onto your property looking to spend money, you are just making the introduction. They are not 'buying a salesperson,' they want your product. Or they don't."

To push ahead and achieve your final goal, you must be ready for rejection. It will happen. But the difference is in how you perceive this rejection. Will you let it defeat you, or can you push ahead no matter what?

Trait #4: Successful Failures Persevere in the Moments of Resistance

How many people do you know start something and give up after a few days? They start to play a new sport but give up if they haven't turned pro in the first three months. They take up painting but drop it after the first attempt because it doesn't look like a Picasso. They leave a sales position after the first day when nobody buys anything on the first twenty calls.

Success is not an overnight event. It takes time, practice, patience and a level of persistent action and resilience before you see results. If you want to break through the barriers of your mind, you must be willing to do whatever it takes. The hard way *is* the way when it comes to handling challenges such as fear, criticism and rejection.

When you are dedicated to the path of failing forward fast, every step carries you closer to your objective. If you get stuck, take time out to assess where you're at and take immediate action when you're clear on your plan.

If you stumble, get up again. When you fail at something for the 100th time, look at the situation and see what you could do differently. Course correct as you move ahead. Take it slow if you must. It isn't a race. In many cases, an overnight success is the culmination of five, ten, or twenty years consistent work.

You will meet with resistance when your objective is worthy of the struggle. Anything easily obtained is rarely valued. The champions who break through meet resistance head on and figure out how to break through it.

To persevere, stay committed to your objective and develop a detailed vision for the life you want to lead.

"There is only one thing that makes a dream impossible to achieve: the fear of failure."

Trait #5: Successful Failures are Committed to Forming New Habits

In Albert Gray's dissertation called "The Common Denominator of Success" he researched the common traits that successful people exhibit. These traits, called "The common denominators of success", are the traits that separate the failures from those who fail and move on to succeed.

In the study, Gray states:

"The common denominator of success—the secret of success of every person who has ever been successful—lies in the fact that he formed the habit of doing things that failures don't like to do."

Take a look around you. Who do you know is living the life you want? If the answer is nobody, keep searching for that person. You must find someone who is performing the habits most people refuse to do. Then, when you find this person, emulate the actions they are taking.

What does this person do consistently? Do they talk about their accomplishments, or simply keep their head down working? How does this person speak? Does she use words of empowerment, and if so, how does she talk? Talk like they do. Has this person failed? How did he handle failing?

Be an observer and a seeker. Look for the successful individual you admire. Copy the actions they take that brings results. Soon, you will experience similar results by building the habits most people refuse to do.

Here are some examples of the habits successful people invest in:

- Time blocking in two hours a day to write your first novel

- Waking up at 5am every morning to work on your future business

- Setting daily priorities and goals

- Scheduling reading as a daily success habit

- Maintaining focus as a key strategy

- Putting an end to mindless shopping or internet surfing

- Committed to mindset development that leads to mind mastery

The key to personal mastery—and conditioning yourself to fail fast—is to be performing tasks that the majority of people won't do.

Trait #6: Successful Failures are Vision Focused on the Big Picture

People who succeed have a clear vision of what they want to achieve, and it drives their perseverance to push past levels of discomfort. High-level achievers can see everything beyond the 'trees in the forest' because they can visualize what needs to be worked on to make the dream happen.

True visionaries can see what lies beyond the struggle. When you visualize what life could be like in the midst of your most difficult struggle, this sparks enthusiasm and passion that drives you forward.

With no vision for your future, you have no plan to get there. Action follows vision. A vision creates reality. You'll always hit your mark when you can see what you're aiming for.

As Helen Keller said:

> *"The only thing worse than being blind is having sight but no vision."*

Start working on your vision right now. Set aside twenty minutes in the morning and evening for this exercise. Sit quietly and imagine the life you are leading. What work are you doing? Where are you living? Who are you with? Where do you want to be a year from now?

See yourself doing the work you love, spending time with people you care about. Create your vision with vivid detail. Leave nothing out of your dream no matter how impossible it appears. Everything is impossible until you start believing it.

Make a firm decision about what you want to be, do, and have. By making a commitment to your willingness to fail, you reduce your fear factor. Resistance is broken by the strength of your mindset. Obstacles are destroyed through your resilience to succeed no matter the price.

The more vivid and detailed the images are, and the stronger you believe in yourself to achieve the impossible, the more driven you will be to work for your goals. A clear vision of where you want to be provides a deeper context for the life you can have.

Trait #7: Successful Failures Focus on a Master Goal

A Master Goal is critical to success. This is a goal so big that at first it appears impossible to reach. Jim Collins, in his book *Built to Last*, calls these goals BHAG (Big Hairy Audacious Goals). According to Collins, a BHAG is a 10+ year visionary goal that describes your envisioned future and is one of the successful habits of both individuals and visionary companies.

I often refer to a BHAG as a master goal.

Your master goal is the BIG goal you commit to that sets your dreams on fire. A BHAG (Master) Goal is built on long-term decisions and milestones set every year.

Les Brown said:

"Your goals are the road maps that guide you and show you what is possible for your life."

Do you have a goal that you've always wanted to achieve? Is it so big it makes you scared to even think about reaching it? Do you believe it's possible to achieve this goal?

Your goals may appear larger than anything you ever dreamed of, but that is how dreams are forged. Nobody ever succeeded in getting what they really wanted by playing it small and safe.

Make your goal your mission. Decide to work for it no matter what happens, no matter how big your challenges or how hard the work. Drive every effort into achieving these goals and stop at nothing until you have reached your goal.

Here are 4 points to consider when developing your master goal:

(1). A master goal is a clear, compelling and achievable goal with a timeframe of 10-20 years

(2). A master goal has clear, compelling milestones set every week, month, and annually.

(3). A master goal clearly reflects your life's mission.

(4). A master goal is big, bold and scary. It makes you fearful to think about it, and this fuels your determination to make it real.

(5). Your master goal is built with absolute necessity. It's your big why. This goal must be achieved no matter what. It provides a reason so compelling that failure is not an option.

Think about this:

In twenty years, where do you see yourself? What kind of person have you developed into because of the success you have achieved?

Now, write down your master goal based on the criteria listed. What is your BHAG? How much time can you commit to this goal every week.

Review your progress at the end of each week. Create daily and weekly target points at the start of each week. You can set monthly goals as well and break it down into your weekly and daily goals.

Your master goal is a lifelong commitment. You will meet obstacles on the way and fail many times but stay fixed on your big why.

Trait #8: Successful Failures Eliminate All Excuses

We make up excuses to justify the reasons why we shouldn't be doing something. This leads into procrastination. Once you buy into the excuse, it becomes automated default verbiage spit out in the moment.

Failure can be misleading. Believing that we can never achieve our goals, we start to formulate the reasoning behind these beliefs. The excuses come up as a means to support our false beliefs. Excuses gives us the justification to stop trying. It makes it easier to surrender and give up. There is no pressure to succeed, and you don't have to stress over failing.

I believe in the motto: "Do nothing, be nothing." An excuse is the lie you tell yourself so you can avoid the shame of looking bad. We must catch ourselves at every chance when using an excuse for not taking intentional action. This starts with, "Oh, I can't because…" or "I'll do it later after I…"

The justifications created that force you to submit to passive inactivity are more damaging than the worst of all failures you could endure. The definition of a true failure isn't someone who tried and never succeeded, but rather someone who never had the courage to try in the first place.

Failing to pursue the things you want in life is a failure in disguise. We use excuses to defend ourselves from the hurts of the world as we build walls that protect limited interests and fragile egos, and to preserve the limited field of vision through which we see the world. Your excuses for not pursuing your dreams might appear to be valid, but under the surface is a path that leads to false reasoning and bitter defeat.

If you really are going to do it later, commit to the action. Set a time and date. Get it done. If not, it becomes another lie that you'll use repeatedly with no intention of following up.

Eliminate your excuses. Recognize the pattern of behavior in you that leans towards failure avoidance and self-sabotaging behavior that feeds into failing.

Your dreams are too important to fall victim to excuses. Start converting excuses into positive words of empowerment. You are not powerless; you wield great power from within.

Trait #9: Successful Failures Focus on Purpose and Meaning

Your sense of working towards a purpose and meaning in life has massive influence towards your "fail fast" attitude. When your purpose drives everything else before it, failure is accepted as a necessary means to achieve the bigger objective. Purpose eliminates fear and prioritizes your actions.

Building a sense of purpose is key to removing self-damaging action carried out through default. How do you build up and expand on your sense of purpose? Throughout this book we will dive deeper into the material that covers gratitude, self-compassion, and a sense of belonging in relationships.

Guided by a purpose in your life, above all strategies, when you believe in what you do, your mission, and the work that must be fulfilled, your drive is an internal engine that cannot be defeated. It is this sense of purpose that drives successful people to do what they do.

Nothing is by accident. Everything happens when a high-level achiever is totally committed to what they are driven to do. It isn't what you get by mastering failure but who you ultimately become.

The 9 Traits Consolidated

Don't worry if you haven't mastered these nine traits yet. This is a work in progress, and you can continue to develop your mindset and build these traits into your life as you work through the material.

Here are the nine traits of successful failures consolidated:

1. Successful Failures Embrace Risk as Part of the Fail Fast Formula

2. Successful Failures Perceive Failure as a Lifelong Strategy

3. Successful Failures Embrace Rejection as a Necessary Element

4. Successful Failures Persevere in the Moments of Resistance

5. Successful Failures are Committed to Forming New Habits

6. Successful Failures are Vision Focused on the Big Picture

7. Successful Failures Focus on a Master Goal

8. Successful Failures Eliminate All Excuses

9. Successful Failures Focus on Purpose and Meaning

Six Limiting Beliefs That Fail You

> *"Don't be afraid to fail. Don't waste energy trying to cover up failure. Learn from your failures and go on to the next challenge. It's ok to fail. If you're not failing, you're not growing."*
>
> **— H. Stanley Judd**

Your beliefs are the pillars of your mindset and set the pace for all future action. Beliefs set the standard for everything that is possible in your life. They are the powerful engines of certainty and deep-rooted convictions. If you want to be the force that controls your destiny, you must recognize both the beliefs that empower you, and, those beliefs limiting your success.

Powerful beliefs open new doors, make the impossible possible, and sets the stage for the life you are preparing to lead. Negative beliefs on the other hand are anchors weighing you down, crushing your motivation, and weakening your determination to blaze forward with intentional action. Instead of embracing failure as a necessary step, your limiting beliefs convince you failure is to be avoided.

If you struggle with fear and are held back by your self-imposed limitations, you could be holding on to old beliefs, making it difficult to push ahead.

You have a choice when it comes to your beliefs. Many beliefs that define your reality have power over you only when you let them take control of your mind. We all have limiting beliefs that we're holding on to when it comes to understanding what failure is really about. But without knowing why you are failing without gains, you will struggle to make forward gains.

For example, if you hold the belief that you are lazy, you will act out this belief and waste quality time Netflix binging or playing video games. Instead of investing time working on your life goals, you throw time away on senseless activities that produce nothing.

When you believe nothing good will ever come of your actions, nothing will ... because your negative beliefs drive everything away. It is the law of attract and repel. You can attract anything you want into your life ... if you believe that it is yours and you deserve it.

Next, I have identified six limiting beliefs that cause many people to fail. You create your own success by structuring your thoughts, habits and beliefs in alignment with a growth mindset. When your beliefs are aligned with your mission, you unlock the door to all the magic.

Limiting Belief #1: If only I had the right skills, education, or privileged background, I would have had a better chance at succeeding.

This limiting belief takes the #1 spot. The limiting belief that your circumstances define you. With this belief, you are led to believe your education defines what you will ultimately succeed at. Your beliefs in family social status is another limiting factor. Were you born into a rich environment, middle-class, poverty, or somewhere in between?

I have seen people from privileged families fail in life when they had every resource available. Yet, someone with a lack of resources—not letting this be a factor in what they could accomplish—went on to create a life of wealth that far surpasses anything they had when starting out. In the end, education and skill plays a role but it doesn't determine the outcome. Only you can do that and what you are willing to believe.

There are a lot of successful entrepreneurs who failed school. This is social proof that we're not defined by the circumstances we are born into. You create your luck by knowing what you want, accepting nothing less than what you're worth, and ignoring the naysayers who tell you to stay where you are.

Regardless of whether it was fifty years ago or today, you are not defined by what you know but what you can do with this knowledge. Your education and training are a jumping-off platform, and that is it. You may not have access to the resources that more privileged people have but believing that is what you need to succeed is your failing point.

"It's not your lack of resources that is the problem but your lack of resourcefulness," motivational guru Tony Robbins has said many times over.

> *"You begin to fly when you let go of self-limiting beliefs and allow your mind and aspirations to rise to greater heights."*
>
> **— Brian Tracy**

Look here at the failures proving everyone wrong:

- Oprah was born into poverty and wore potato sacks for clothes.

- Colonel Sanders slept in his car trying to sell his fried chicken franchise living off of a dwindling retirement income.

- Larry Ellison of Oracle dropped out of college and then university, starting up a business that almost failed before he mortgaged his house to stay afloat.

- Walt Disney quit school, was fired for "lack of imagination," and lost everything when he came up with an idea for Mickey Mouse on the train.

- JK Rowling was almost homeless, on welfare, and a single mother when she was writing the first Harry Potter book.

Your education, background, previous training and all of that can be blown away in a moment. When you decide to do something and make a commitment to really go for it, nothing can stand between you and what you want.

Throughout this book, I am going to destroy your limiting beliefs so that they never interfere with your *Fail Big* wins again.

Limiting Belief #2: My life is at the mercy of external events

Your mindset is at the heart of learning how to turn failing into successful advantage. Being connected—and in alignment with your attitude and mindset towards failing—is your ability to take responsible action.

At the end of the day, no matter what happens to you, this is no reason for you to be beaten by the circumstances of the world. Even if you end up losing everything, the one thing that cannot be taken away from you is your power to make a choice. You must ask yourself at any given time, "What can I do right now to gain control of this situation?"

Viktor Frankl, the holocaust survivor who spent four years surviving in the Nazi deathcamps, said:

> *"Everything can be taken from a person but one thing: the last of human freedoms - to choose one's attitude in any given set of circumstances, to choose one's own way."*

First, you can only control your controllables. What happens around you—or to you—is not entirely your fault. But you are responsible for how you react to these external events.

Here is what you can control:

- Daily habits

- What you eat

- Learning new skills

- Developing your mindset

- Key decisions

- How to spend your time

- Your reaction to another person's anger or attitude

There isn't much you can do if your company decided to let you go because they are making employee cuts. You can complain to your friends and family, picket outside the building of your ex-employer, and try to get your job back if you really miss it that much.

If you're in a position where you feel powerless to do something, it could be that you can't do much at all. Focus your energy on the actions that can improve your situation for the better, and not make it worse.

Ask yourself, "What choice do I have here? How do I want to handle this? Will I cry and make noise or take a positive approach and work towards something better?"

People fail in many ways, but it isn't the kind of failure you are thinking about. You might have a relationship that fails, lose lots of money, your job is gone, or the goal you've been working towards for the past five years has suddenly dried up and is out of reach.

There are events in your life beyond your control. Your strategy should be deciding what you should focus on and what you need to let go of.

Limiting Belief #3: Failing is avoidable (if you play it safe)

Are you someone who minimizes risk by doing as little as possible? Do you expend energy trying to steer clear of disaster by playing it safe? One of the biggest beliefs that fail you is this: *The less risk I buy into, the greater will be my chances of getting by without losing anything.*

When you avoid taking any risks at all, you are saying NO to pushing forward towards your goal.

Have you heard of Bronnie Ware? Bronnie Ware is an Australian nurse who spent several years working in palliative care, caring for patients in the last 12 weeks of their lives. She recorded their dying epiphanies and published her observations in a book called *The Top Five Regrets of the Dying.*

Of the five regrets the patients had, the regret most prevalent among them was:

I wish I'd had the courage to live a life true to myself, not the life others expected of me.

With no hope of their dreams coming to fruition, these people lived playing it safe and never truly performed at the level they could have. Most people had to die knowing that it was due to choices they had made, or not made, that would become their legacy.

If you fear failing, I want you to think about this: Next week, you become sick. Confined to a bed because you are too ill to move, you are placed in a position to reflect on your own life, what you accomplished, and everything you didn't. Visualizing this moment, what are your final regrets?

Now, come back to this moment.

Reflect on this truth: You and I will die someday, and it may be sooner than you think. What would you do from this day forward to your last if you could do anything? What will be the one choice you make, the risk you take, that shifts your destiny from where you are now to where you want it to be?

What will be the end result if you don't make this happen? How will you feel at the end of your days? Like many people that have been there, you could end up regretting the things you always wanted to do but never did.

Don't let it happen.

Failure *is* avoidable. You can avoid it, minimize your risks, and play it safe so you don't lose anything precious. But what are you losing? Money, pride, embarrassment or your false self-esteem?

You won't live forever, and you won't live for long, but what you decide now, by embracing your greatest moment of failing and being totally okay with it, will be the defining factor in the kind of life you lead. We can't sit home every night watching Netflix pretending that everything is okay when life is moving past us and our dreams are dying one more day at a time.

As Bronnie Ware interviewed the dying in their final moments and revealed to the world their last crushing failure … the failure of never having truly lived, this is your wakeup call. The time is now, and the day is today.

You are alive, and you can choose to do whatever you wish. If fear holds you back now, do you think it will be any better in five, ten or thirty years from now when the last fear you are holding on to is that of dying? Trust me. If you live this life like the wild ride it is, pursuing and finally living out your dreams, when the end of days comes, you will be looking forward to moving into the next adventure.

Limiting Belief #4: Once a failure, always a failure…

This is a belief centred around sabotaging your future. If you fail at winning a race, do you never race again? Fail at a test, do you stop taking tests? Fail at marriage, do you never date again? This is your negative internal monologue feeding you lies.

You can silence this voice right now. If you ever tell yourself this again, it is a lie. Failures rise up from the bottom of the worst bottom you can imagine. Need more proof? Keep reading this book because I provide enough examples to expose this limiting belief for what it really is.

Limiting Belief #5: I have no talent, skill, creativity or special abilities

If you tell yourself these things, yes, you're right. Talent is the result of hard work. Some people are born with natural talent, but most skills are improved with tough learning. In fact, hard work beats talent every day. One of my favorite speakers is Gary Vaynerchuk. Why? He doesn't let people get away with feeding their ego excuses. He tells it like it is and what he says is, "If you are relying on talent alone to succeed, you will be disappointed."

Talent is second to nothing when it comes to success. There are a lot of talented people out there who haven't worked hard enough and so they have the talent with nothing else to show for it.

Creativity, while it can be an inborn trait, is a skill too. Your skill can be learned. This limiting belief is what fails many people and holds them back. It is part of the fixed mindset. You want the growth mindset that states:

"I can have anything I want, learn anything I need to, and succeed with hard work beyond whatever talent I have."

Never let anyone tell you that you can't succeed if you don't have the education or the skill. If you need training or skill strengthening, you get to work and learn what you need to.

Before I started writing books, I didn't know very much about book production. But I committed to learning everything I needed to publish my own works. I read books on publishing, took a few courses, and just went for it. I could have sat back and said, "I know nothing about this, so why try?"

When you have desire, and your passion is stronger than anything else, you have no barriers holding you back.

Limiting belief #6: "If I haven't succeeded by now, I never will…"

You can work hard for ten or twenty years at something and not get to where you want to be with the success you were expecting. To become good at something, it can take a short time or decades. But it isn't the end result you should be focused on.

How many paintings did Picasso create before he liked what he was producing? How many shots did Jordan take at the hoop before he made it to the NBA? How many novels did Dan Brown write before his books started to sell?

When you believe in what you love to do, you'll work on this day by day. Obviously, you won't become an NBA player if you're still practicing shots into your middle age, but you'll never get anywhere if you give up too soon or start thinking, *I'll never get there.*

What you <u>believe</u> is who you <u>become</u>.

You decide at what point you are ready to give it up. But understand what you're giving up. Does this mean you're casting aside your dream to settle for a job that you never wanted? Are you prepared to live a life of mediocre existence because you couldn't stick it out and focus on the small day-by-day action steps?

Thomas Edison, who failed thousands of times in creating his inventions, said:

> *"Many of life's failures are people who did not realize how close they were to success when they gave up."*

You might be close. Give it another week. Another day. Keep pushing harder for one more hour. Don't give yourself permission to be defeated. Turn this limiting belief into an inspiring mantra:

> *"I'm not where I want to be yet, but I'm a lot closer than I was last year."*

If you are consistent in your actions, this is true. Small actions taken daily count towards the big picture. This goes for writing your first five thousand words of a book, shooting 20 hoops a day, or running 2 km each morning. Your success is a measure of these actions taken consistently. Failure is not final until we stop short of that finish line.

Now, you might have more than six limiting beliefs. Regardless, you can start today to make a shift in your beliefs.

In my book <u>Drive Your Destiny</u>, I discuss the power for beliefs and provide a six-step formula for changing a belief.

Change Your Limiting Beliefs: A Six-Step Process

Here are six steps you can take to begin changing anything in your life. Keep in mind that this takes time and you won't always succeed by doing something once or twice. Like any habit, you have to keep at it.

Step 1: Identify the belief you want to change. This is the first step to taking positive action. You can only change something if you know what you need to change, and why you want to change it.

Core negative beliefs that make you feel inferior, inadequate, or worthless should be first on your list. Why hang on to your painful thoughts any longer? This is a tough step for most people. We have been feeding into our pain for so long it starts to appear normal.

I can assure you that in working through your pain, and recognizing the negative beliefs you created about yourself, your life will begin to take a dramatic shift.

Here are some examples of beliefs you may have about yourself. See if you recognize any of these:

"Everything bad that happens to me is my fault."

"I feel like I am less competent than everyone else when it comes to success or getting ahead in life."

"I feel like a failure or a 'nobody' when in the presence of other people who are obviously better than me."

"I have no qualities worth talking about that anyone would be interested in."

"I should be perfect at all times. I have to show people I am perfect."

"I am inherently flawed."

You might have a number of faulty beliefs about yourself that have disempowered you throughout most of your life. I know I did before I worked to turn them around. The key is to recognize what they are. Some are buried deep. Others are more noticeable and are running through your mind a hundred times a day. They feel so normal that you don't question their validity.

Take time to write them out and list as many as you can. You can start with parts of the short list above that apply and add to it with your own negative beliefs. Pay attention to the beliefs that target your self-esteem and devalue your worth.

Step 2: Disempower the old belief by introducing doubt and uncertainty. It is time to take a stand and question your belief, analyzing it under a mental microscope through strict analysis. It is time to put your beliefs on trial.

You are going to question your beliefs, attack their vulnerability, tear down their walls, and weaken their structure. If a belief has been built on lies and falsehoods, it will not stand up to the scrutiny of your attack.

Go deep with your ideas and push back hard. Ask pertinent questions that disengage the power your belief has over you. Tell yourself that this is not a reality you choose to believe in anymore. Disown it completely. Choose to believe in something else. This is when your mind makes a shift toward reframing what it has been trained to accept.

Step 3: Reframe the new belief while disempowering the old one. Full of fear, self-doubt, and lacking confidence, we can easily slip back into old patterns of defeat. We can convince ourselves that negative beliefs are true.

When you decide to replace your old beliefs, you are making a firm commitment: *I refuse to feel this way anymore. From now on, I am going to reject all negative thoughts.* If you do this enough, you will be thinking and behaving differently.

Step 4: Visualize the person you will become once you have created a new belief. Visualize yourself behaving differently, taking new and decisive actions, and pushing through your fear instead of being blocked by it.

See yourself overcoming the obstacles that, until now, have been holding you back. Imagine the new way of life that waits for you on the other side of conquering your fears.

Then, visualize the steps that you would need to take to make this transition. What could you do right now to begin building momentum? How would you have to think and act to achieve an outcome that is seemingly beyond your reach or capability? Once you have the clear answer, it is time to start being that person.

Step 5: Reinforce this new belief, taking further repetitive action towards making it real. Now that you have a solid idea of the changes you want, start by supporting your new belief. Take immediate action and reframe your old belief with the new one.

If you tear down the old belief but do nothing to replace it, you'll eventually resort to that old destructive way of thinking. When this happens, just remember what your replacement belief is and continue to reinforce it over and over. Such reinforcement has to be done consistently in order to succeed.

Try writing out ten of your favorite quotes. Utilize the power of positive words and affirmations. Repeat these several times a day. It will be uncomfortable at first, but be persistent.

The more you use words of positive power, the faster you can shift your beliefs to accepting what you are saying and thinking. Persistence and consistency are the keys. Soon you will be able to pull out your positive mental toolbox and use it to overpower negative thoughts and words.

Self-conversation is a powerful tool. Your negative beliefs used this tool against you for many years. Now you know that you can choose thoughts that support your new belief. Give your new belief lots of encouragement and support. Repeat it as many times as you need to. Convince yourself that it is true!

Step 6: Follow-up with action. In this final stage, you are going to continually strengthen your belief through convincing evidence. You will alter your actions and behaviors to align with the new belief as it starts planting roots deep in your subconscious.

It is important to reinforce the new beliefs on a continual basis. Create the beliefs you want to have. Do not settle on thoughts that devalue you.

Once a year, you could give yourself a small test to see where you are with your beliefs and analyze whether they are consistent with your desires and purpose.

You may discover, as I have, that there are new discrepancies with your current beliefs and values. If so, you can always update your belief system every year, making subtle changes here and there, adjusting your course in order to stay on track.

Making a Difference

You can change your beliefs about failing. Just because you had a string of failures growing up, suffered setbacks, or you lost everything after taking a risk to succeed, these events do not define what you're capable of now.

The only moment that matters is now. You can make a difference in your future. You can make a difference in how you act today. When you move forward, it fills you up with creative energy. Your motivation comes from taking charge of the moment and not accepting life as it is but, rather, making it the way you want.

Fail Big Reflection

What are your limiting beliefs? How have your limiting beliefs shaped your experiences up to now?

Visualize your life from now on and the change you can begin to implement when you put an end to the limiting beliefs you have about failing.

What is something you have been working on for a long time? Measure your progress now compared to last month, last year or ten years ago. How close are you to reaching your goal?

When your limiting beliefs are crowding your mind, think about this quote from American self-help author Robert Collier:

"Success is the sum of small efforts, repeated day in and day out."

Make the difference. Crush your limiting beliefs.

Taking Extreme Responsibility for Your Fails

"On any team, in any organization, all responsibility for success and failure rests with the leader. The leader must own everything in his or her world. There is no one else to blame. The leader must acknowledge mistakes and admit failure."

In this chapter, we talk about owning responsibility and what that means when it comes to failing big. It is not about finding fault or hunting down a scapegoat. This strategy that so many organizations and individuals are used to participating in can only end one way: Failure for both parties.

Let's focus in on what it means to take responsibility—extreme responsibility—so that you can support people when a mistake is made, or a more serious failure has happened.

This means owning your end, when necessary, and taking the blame even when it wasn't all your doing. By taking *extreme ownership*, not only are you owning your own failures but, you are in a position to do something about it.

Solutions can only be presented after we have identified the problem, what went wrong, and how to correct it so that same situation doesn't happen again. If it does happen again, you drill down deeper to identify the core issue.

So, what is extreme ownership? In a nutshell, it is owning your actions. It is owning the total result of your actions, even if other people are following your direction.

"Extreme Ownership is the practice of owning everything in your world, to an extreme degree. It means you are responsible for not just those tasks which you directly control, but for all those that affect whether or not your mission is successful."

— Joe Taylor, The Conductor Blog

You can boil this down to employees in a business, members of a SEAL team, or your own family members. When something bad happens and everyone is looking for someone to blame, you are asking yourself, "What could I have done differently in this situation? What role did my actions [or lack of] make this failure happen? What can we—as a team—take away from this and use as an extreme learning principle?

By failing to take responsibility for ones' actions, this is extreme failure on many levels. You set yourself up to continue failing. This is why many organizations, companies, and even families break apart. Everyone becomes fearful of owning their part. The consequences of getting into trouble, losing the power of ego,

Extreme Ownership is the pillar of a leader. When it comes to failing big, it is the biggest step you can take to accepting your fails, learning from it, and adapting so the next attempt has a better result. It still might not turn out the exact way you were expecting, but by stepping in you are doing what it takes to make a difference.

As the book of the same name implies, without taking Extreme Ownership for the mistakes and failures of your team, your company, your family, and holding yourself accountable, there isn't always a winning solution. You will continue to drag yourself through the mud and everyone else will go down with you. The biggest shift in any organization always happens when the anchors weighing down the success of the company are recognized and cut loose.

Now, you may not be a hard-combatted Navy SEAL, but this is irrelevant. You, me, and everyone around you—from day to day—are involved in interactions, relationships, events, decision-making, and participate to some degree in the success or failure of our own lives.

At the very core, you are most likely integrated with a group in business or, you are in charge of taking care of a family. Extreme Ownership exists within each of us and, it is up to you and I, to exercise our *Extreme Ownership* in the people we influence: At work, at home, and in our communities, staying true to your ownership is the pillar of character

But before we dive into the traits of EO, let's take a look at what it isn't. We can learn a lot from the failures, mistakes and lack of ownership people displayed in both their professional and personal lives.

Take a look around you at the people you meet, work with or have discussion with every day. How many people can you say you know display the traits of a leader prepared to accept failure. Who do you know is ready to FAIL BIG so they can start living the life they are destined for? How many people are ready to go the distance and do whatever it takes to take extreme responsibility for the course of their lives.

Now, most importantly, what are you prepared to do to live a life of extreme ownership? What does this mean to you? What would you have to change to begin this way of action today?

As the author of *Extreme Ownership*—Jocko Willink—explains in his teachings, one of the chief blocks to extreme ownership is the fixed mindset. I discussed this critical trait earlier in this book and we know that, before anything begins, you must be willing to break this obstacle first. We have found that, without your growth mindset leading the way, none of the other strategies in this book or any other will actually work.

To change and thrive, you must be ready to learn and take ownership of your life.

The material I have been teaching you up to this point has all been pointing towards this: Responsibility. Too be more exact, taking extreme responsibility and not allowing yourself to buy into excuses or laziness as a way out. As soon as you do, your victim mentality takes over and you're back to fighting a losing battle: The battle with your own mind that refuses to let go.

When you live the *Fail Big* lifestyle, and use extreme ownership—taking full responsibility—for your life as the ultimate growth mindset tool, you step up your game to the highest level. Not only do you hold yourself accountable but, you hold others accountable for their actions, too. Now, we can't force people to see things our way, but we can lead by example. If they choose to join you or not, that's on them.

What does it mean to live a life of total responsibility and take extreme ownership of your life and your destiny?

Here are the 9 lessons I have built out for this chapter as a final lesson in showing you how to begin your Fail Big journey and exponentially increase your success as you fail ahead.

Taking Extreme Responsibility: 5-Point Action Checklist

If you are to live a life of extreme responsibility, there are 7 points you should remember. When it comes to Failing Big, you will accelerate your growth and success exponentially by adhering to a set of principles. You can't take responsibility in one area of your life while ignoring the other. It won't work, and the unbalance will shift out of your favor.

(1) The Focus is Progress, Not Perfection

In any organization, within families and for every individual, mistakes are made and failure happens. But three steps forward, two steps back is not a setback. That is one step forward. And the other two steps that you messed up on are the lessons you learned on the way.

The progress made is your success. Shift your perspective so that you can see the effort you are making. Shooting for perfection is establishing failure from the outset. You fail because you can't finish your project. You fail because you get stuck for fear of moving ahead. You fail because you can't see the forest through the trees.

You fail when perfection becomes the goal and not the progress made.

If you're in charge of a team, or you are the head of your household, you are the mentor others look up to. We are all leaders in the sense that, we lead by example. Drop your expectations. They will cripple you. If you set a goal to earn $100,000 a year, and you hit $80k, up $20k from your previous salary, that is progress.

Locking your mind into "black and white" thinking fails you for two reasons.

1. Most people rarely celebrate their wins. They hit the goal and then fixate on the next level

2. If they fail to hit the target they set, but only achieve 30% instead of 50%, their black and white mindset fixes this as a failure.

A 5% improvement is still a gain. It's a positive gain. For example:

1. Your daughter brings home a report card and her overall grades are 5% higher than last term. (and not the A+ average you were hoping for).

2. You sell 5% more product than last year. (and not the 20% increase you wanted).

3. You lose 5% of your body fat (and not the 10% you wanted).

There are instances where failure is not accepted, and these could be life-threating circumstances. But most people are not dealing with dangerous circumstances.

Step back and stop taking things so seriously. I'm not suggesting you lower your standards. You can have big goals. But failing to hit that goal the first time leads to disappointment and failure to see the win.

(2) Communicate Expectations Clearly, and Eliminate Confusion

I sincerely believe that most people try their best to do a good job. We don't always get the results or positive outcome that is expected of us, and it's harder when expectations are not communicated.

If you are responsible for delivering these expectations, be clear on what the mission objective is. When I say "mission", I am referring to the aim of the project or goal you are trying to reach.

Most people fail because they are not aware of the objectives or expectations. Leaving out key details that is needed to get the job done results in…the job not getting done.

Too add to injury, the person who fails to deliver is blamed for not following through. If you give someone directions to reach a certain destination, they need those directions to be clear. If not, they end up some place else.

(3) Blame is Not an Option

This is the #1 reason 97% of the people are afraid to fail. Didn't someone always get mad when you made a critical error? Our system is set up to "punish" for getting it wrong. Blaming others when it goes wrong is the sign of a weak leader.

I worked in a company that operated this way. When something went wrong, the person responsible was pulled into a room and ridiculed…often in front of others. Bad form. This happens more than you think. In 90% of the cases, the manager is to "blame" if anyone. This is why the definition of "manager" has a negative stigma. Most managers are seen as "blame seekers" who hunt down the party responsible.

Does it matter whose fault it is? The only thing that matters is correction is made to reduce the failure rate. Have you ever been in a situation when something went wrong, you knew it was your doing, but you stayed quiet as they searched for the guilty? How did it feel? Chances are you stayed quiet, hoping they wouldn't find out and move on.

I did this years ago. Only the blame fell on someone else that wasn't responsible. But do you notice how everyone becomes obsessed with finding who did it. And then what? Punish that person so they never do it again? Meanwhile, this sends a message: If you fail, we will come after you.

Blame is not an option. It holds everything up. Nobody learns from it. It breeds fear into everyone.

Fear fuels the fear of failure. And the fear of failing is the reason I write this book: So, you can stop being scared and learn to love failing like you never have before!

(4) Empower People to Fail Big and Admit Failure

I tell people I'm leading that it's okay to fail. I let them know that there are no points taken away for dropping the ball. When someone joins a company and it is their first week, they are given a long list of rules to follow. The list is very intense and, although it means well as a method to set up employee expectations, it also intimidates.

This new person is brought on board and then warned that if you do A, B or C, you'll be brought up on a performance evaluation. Following this, possible termination if your performance has not improved.

What happens then? The employee is walking on egg shells afraid of making a mistake. When he or she does, they think twice before admitting it. A company has to set expectations but in doing so, they outline the risk involved when you don't measure up.

We can't make companies or individuals change their policies, but you can encourage people that failing is okay. You will learn as you fail, and this opens the doorway for better opportunity.

The second part to this is admitting fault. Making an error that brings failure to your team or family is a hard step to process. You let others down. They are counting on you and, you didn't hold up your end. How do I admit failing without bringing embarrassment to myself?

People appreciate honesty, even if they aren't happy with your mistake. But what is less tolerable would be the circumstances of holding back and not revealing the truth. This is at the heart of extreme ownership. When you have to admit in front of your peers, manager or your friends that you failed them.

Then, you move on to the solution. How can I take a different action next time? Your supporters will give great ideas for succeeding if you let them in. But shut people out and hide the truth, and you get help from nobody.

Extreme responsibility is admitting when you let yourself down and in doing so, let the team down. But from there, you can rebuild, and you haven't lost trust. By admitting failure, you establish trust, you don't lose it. We are wired to think differently.

If I fail, I must be a failure.

Winners can admit defeat and make a comeback to try again. Losers blame the winners for cheating and walk away without ever coming back.

If you're in a leadership role, a parent or a teacher (and most people are in at least one) the best approach to take is this: Reach Down to Help Others Up, Don't Hammer Them Down. Empower people to take ownership no matter the role they are playing.

I have seen children take greater ownership of fault then adults. Everyone can identify with this lesson and if it's learned early in life, imagine the impact you can carry forward in the years to come.

(5) Initiate Problem-Solving Communication

Blame and criticism doesn't solve anything. Its intention is to deflect the fault onto someone so everyone else can rest easier. The people, teams, companies and families who succeed are in the practice of embracing problem-solving solutions as the only logical step forward.

Criticism, labeling, and finding fault is destructive, not constructive. You set the stage for failing hard, not failing forward.

Problem-solving communication is an open discussion that makes people relaxed and confident, knowing that they can voice an option or initiate conversation that will be heard. This sends the message that, not just any one person has all the answers. You can help people on your team or in your own family to embrace the moment and share the solutions to a problem or be willing to try something new even if it means they could fail at it.

Taking Responsibility for Failure: Building Character Traits

By evading responsibility, you think you're escaping punishment, embarrassment or losing face. Yes, you could be avoiding the backlash. But you pay for this with a heavy price later. Failure and owning up to your fails are not an easy path to take again and again.

It takes a commitment to character in order to show up and be the best. We know there is a risk in not owning your shit. But, what is the risk? It's not about avoiding getting the axe or saving your ego from embarrassment.

Striving to **take responsibility for your** life and ownership of **your mistakes** is worth it for five specific reasons:

(1). People respect you…even if they hate you.

Nothing gains respect or builds trust faster than raw honesty. By opening up, you have nothing to hide. Your ability to take ownership of your actions is the #1 pathway to accelerated growth. Not just for you, but the people around you.

(2). Encourages others to take ownership.

As we discussed in this section, taking responsibility is a big leap. But it is the only risk you must take. And in doing so, you empower the people around you to take intentional action.

Your positive reinforcement that failing is completely acceptable, tells the people around you "Hey, you're allowed to make mistakes. Go out there and do your best and when you fall down, get up again. Keep falling down but keep getting up."

(3). Builds a Well-Disciplined and Confident Mindset

Your mindset is a garden, and you are the master gardener. You must be ready to remove the weeds from your own mind so it isn't at the mercy of weak habits. By taking complete ownership, you essentially take ownership of your mind. This is the elimination of fear. The removal of uncertainty.

A confident mindset can own anything. You won't hesitate to admit defeat, and you will put yourself in a position of healthy empowerment. People who can admit failure to another come across as honest, trustworthy, and dependable.

Ask yourself: "What is the type of character I want to build?" Then, use extreme responsibility to build that character.

(4). Break Fear and Build the Foundation for Exponential Growth

Everyone dreams of a better life. Doing things better, being more productive, becoming a better person, or improving our attitude that in effect improves happiness. This is exponential growth and there is nothing to build this faster than taking full ownership for your life. By owning up, you level up. That's it.

If you want to develop the skills to handle failure, admit your failure and you've taken a huge leap forward. While most people are busy blaming and complaining, you are owning and taking massive action.

By breaking your fear, you are undefeatable. The "secret" people spend years searching for can be defined here:

"Breaking the fear of failure is not a mystery. You don't need therapy, books, or expensive coaching to achieve this. You only need the willingness to step up and own your responsibility. No blaming, no complaining. The solution-focused individual becomes master of the mind as soon as they shift focus towards ownership of their actions."

Failure vs. Success:
a Shift in Perspective

> *"Forget about the consequences of failure. Failure is only a temporary change in direction to set you straight for your next success."*

> **— Denis Waitley**

The line between failing and success is not a multi-directional path; it is the same road. Your success is linked to the amount of failure you're willing to endure.

The #1 reason most people fail isn't because of the mistakes they've made along the way but, rather, the lack of chances they took. It is the mistakes you are not willing to make that defeat you. It is the risk you avoid that leads to your long-term failure and not the other way around.

By putting failure into perspective, we can condition the way we think and feel about failing. Many people are haunted by the fears and threats of voices from the past that say, "Be careful! You don't know what you're getting into."

Two people can set out on the same path and end up at different destinations. On the way, both men are met with unseen challenges. Obstacles that block their performance or threaten to hold them back. Same path, but one man makes it to the end and the other gives up and heads back to the start. He tries to find another path that gets him to the finish line, an easier road that is not as challenging, but every road is the same: filled with fears, risk and obstacles that he must conquer before moving on.

Frustrated and hopeless, he gives up, unable to move on.

The other man meets the same obstacles along the way. There are times when he gets stuck for days, unable to move ahead, and he just sits for hours thinking about a solution that takes him to the next phase. This man has something that the other doesn't. His attitude is different. He believes that the only way through is to keep pushing forward to the end. He decided from the beginning that no matter what happens, he will succeed in spite of the challenges thrown at him.

He meditates on problems and prays for guidance. Somehow, he will make it. He doesn't know how, but the destination can only be reached if he moves ahead. He knows that by going back to the beginning, every road will be met with similar challenges.

When the man returns home and meets his friend who he started out with, his friend asks, "How did you get to the end of the journey and I didn't?"

The man replies, "Simple. I followed one philosophy. I just kept moving forward and I never gave up."

It's easy to look at failure as an enemy that hides in the shadows, waiting for the opportunity to jump in and ruin your life.

In many cultures, we are told from the beginning that failure is something to avoid. If you fail, you must have done something wrong. If you fail, there will be consequences. If you fail, you will be punished, not pass go, and forget about collecting anything. Only winners get to reap the benefits. Prizes are not given for second place.

To avoid these consequences at any cost, we avoid doing anything that involves risk. Play it safe, keep your head down, and you'll make it through. This leads to the "life in a bubble" way of life. You want to get ahead, to succeed in life, but nobody gets what they want unless they are willing to pay the price for it.

And the **risk is scary**.

In fact, the true reason we are afraid to fail is because the experience of failing has been met with criticism ("Oh look, you did it again!"), harsh warnings ("Be careful you don't muck it up again,") and the possibility of reprimand. If this is what awaits you on the other side of fear, is it any wonder we would rather stay on the side of the river that is the safest?

> *"Success is stumbling from failure to failure with no loss of enthusiasm."*
>
> ## — Winston Churchill

I want to define the difference between success and failure. You think they are separate identities and that one has nothing to do with the other. But, in fact, one cannot survive without the other.

Staying committed to a lifetime of personal growth is about being in this for the long term. If you are focused on short-term wins and quick fixes, failing forward probably isn't for you. When the rubber meets the road, you find out what you're made of. Going into business for yourself, becoming an entrepreneur, or getting married are long-term commitments. And with any of these there is a chance of it failing.

The people who fail, and plan to fail, are the ones who go into a situation half-heartedly. They have back doors built for escape and can be heard saying, "Well, if it doesn't work out I'll just..."

When you build an escape route into your plan, you're planning to fail at some point. You just want the fall to be less painful than it has to be. Your "fall back" plan is failure expectation. There is no guarantee that your business will succeed, but if you go into it with the attitude that "Failure is inevitable, so I need a backup" you are going to be making decisions built from fear.

To succeed, you must be committed to making it work, even when it is broken. Relationships are not perfect, and most break down, but even then, you only fail if you learn nothing and keep making the same mistakes again and again.

You go into a relationship and make the same mistakes in the second marriage as you do the first. That ends and you take your issues that ruined the first two and carry them into all future relationships. The result is a lifetime of perpetual failure. This is what I refer to as the broken loop cycle of perpetual failure. You continue to do again and again what you've always done and, as a result, you get the same outcome.

I have a friend who has gone into business three times for himself. All three businesses failed. But that is not the problem. A lot of people fail at business over and over and over until they make it. They try something different and fail when it doesn't work. But when you make the same errors that caused you to fail in the first place, you are not failing forward, you're just failing. Eventually, you run out of resources and people are tired of working with you.

We can see examples of people failing all around us. The manager that gets passed around from department to department. The business owner that goes into debt ... again ... borrowing from friends and family, never repaying those debts, and destroying trust along the way. The partners that fight over the same issues but never resolve anything. A friend's health that continues to decline because she is eating all the foods the doctor warned her about.

The real failures in these stories fail not from the circumstances or external conditions but because of who they are. The values, beliefs and actions driven by these values and beliefs. If you are out to make a quick dollar, you might resort to salesy scams to rip people off. But your long-term growth will never happen.

Reshaping Negative Experiences

Throughout this book, my goal is to reshape how you view failure. If you are like many people, failure has always been an event you should avoid. If you are failing—in business, in school, or in life— it doesn't mean you are a total failure. It could be a sign that you are doing something that isn't working.

The experience is about testing, failing, and testing again and you continue to push ahead as you grow through your fails. You can always change the road you're on at any time. You can take a different course of action and change your behavior. You can develop new habits (more on this later). You can shift your attitude and perspective towards failing.

Failing Your Way to Success

This is a book that will show you how to succeed as a failure; it's not about avoiding it so you can feel more successful. My philosophy is, win or lose, you have to be taking some form of risk to get to where you want to be. While other people are taking it easy, kicking back and drinking away the weekend, you are hunkered down somewhere building something that will last.

In this book, I want to teach you what failure is, what it isn't, and how we can pillar our mistakes, so they help us to become more successful for tomorrow.

Uncertainty is a part of the process. Not knowing what to do next is part of the game. Starting over again when you lose your best hand is the way it is most of the time. But what matters is you are always ready to play, no matter what.

Failure is your best friend and will never lie to you. You cannot fail when you have the attitude of a winner. A true champion says, "I didn't do so well today. This was my worst performance day yet. But tomorrow, I'll come back here and train harder, learn harder, push harder."

A mindset with this kind of attitude can never be beaten. Most people are defeated, not by the world around them but the world within them. You are defeated by your own hand in the end. You will always be defeated by who you are and not who somebody else is.

Blame is for the weak. By taking full responsibility for your own life, everything around you changes. It becomes less painful to hold on. It shapes your perception of how we should be. You let go of false perceptions and entitlement.

Entitlement, the belief that the world or your parents or your spouse owes you something because you are so special, must be broken. You cannot move forward if you are holding on to your beliefs about entitlement. I believe it is best to focus on this idea right now:

"I am responsible for everything I decide to do. I may not be responsible for what happens to me, or around me, but how I react to it and how I choose to live with it is mine."

Life is difficult.

The road is not easy. If you're in the mindset that you're doing something wrong because you've run into difficulty, listen to what I am telling you: If it is difficult, and you are making mistakes along the way, you are on the right path.

You have permission to fail, make mistakes and mess up in every way possible. Go ahead. Fail fast and make a comeback. Fall down hard and get back up.

People who expect it to be easy are setting themselves up for failing the hard way. When they run up against an obstacle, they are usually the first to give up. A problem comes up that they can't solve? They watch TV instead. If they take a risk and miss the shot, they storm off the court complaining the game must be rigged somehow, never to go back to the game.

Life is difficult, as Scott Peck said to us in *The Road Less Travelled*. The issue is we want it to be easy. We use escape tactics to evade responsibility and blame someone else when it doesn't work. All of this is the true path to failing hard.

The difference between success and failure: **Success is the result of having failed many times.** Success is your attitude towards failing and embracing this as the necessary way. Failing is the only way, the hard way, and the best way you know to reach the summit of your dreams. It is the runner that goes that extra distance when everyone else has fallen behind and quit.

You can go fast, go slow, but don't stop.

> *"It does not matter how slowly you go*
> *so long as you do not stop."*

— Confucius (551–479 BC), philosopher

Fail Big Action Plan

How many failures are you willing to endure? What does it mean for you to go the extra mile? What action will you take the next time you fail?

Embrace the Fear of Risk

"Twenty years from now you will be more disappointed by the things you didn't do than by the ones you did. So throw off the bowlines, sail away from the safe harbor, catch the trade winds in your sails. Explore. Dream. Discover."

— **Mark Twain**

In 1974, a young programmer named Paul Allen stumbled across an article in *Popular Electronics,* advertising the Altait 8800— the first Microprocessor—on its front cover. Paul showed the article to Bill Gates and they came up with the idea to develop an implementation of BASIC (**Beginners' All-purpose Symbolic Instruction Code**) for the system.

Bill Gates didn't hesitate, as he was known to be a hyperactive go-getter and action taker. He contacted Altair's manufacturer, MITS (Micro Instrumentation and Telemetry Systems), and offered to demonstrate the implementation for a system that they had not yet even built. But that didn't matter.

Gates and Allen made the decision, bluffed about what they really had, and set out to create the system within eight weeks with the help of a systems engineer named Monte Davidoff.

The risk paid off, the interpreter for the system worked, and MITS agreed to distribute Altair BASIC.

Bill Gates then made another risky decision: he quit Harvard and set out with Paul Allen to start up Micro-soft (later to become Microsoft). This was possible with the money made from the Altair BASIC.

Bill Gates is not a stranger to risk-taking, but the lesson he has to teach us is grounded in the actions taken to build something that the world needed. But Bill Gates admits that he was plagued by worry and anxiety. Failure was always imminent, especially when companies he idolized—**Digital Equipment and Wang**—went bankrupt.

Bill Gates had anxiety about running a large company, but as he has proven, there is risk involved in taking risks. There is risk involved in not taking risks, too. You must decide for yourself if the next decision you make is a step towards your dreams.

Opportunity only presents itself once. You might pass on a chance where you have to decide in the moment if this is what you're going to do. If risk is what you fear because of the potential loss, then you must be ready to accept the consequences.

"You will never regret the failures you've had in trying. But you will regret your failure in never having tried at all."

As Bill said, *"To win big, you sometimes have to take big risks."* But you don't have to take big risks or gamble away your life-savings. Your level of risk must be in alignment with the goal you're aiming for. The bigger the risk, the more intense your resistance to failure is.

Risk Evaluation: Play it Safe or Play to Win

The biggest risk you could be taking is the risk of playing it safe to avoid making a mistake. When we play our cards so carefully as to avoid losing the game, we fold our hand by default.

It doesn't matter if you lose. It hurts, and you might suffer a loss, but what's important is, you show up to play. You come to the game prepared to give it your best. You don't have to be the best athlete on the field to win, you only need the willingness to play hard. Play to win but embrace your losses is an experience all successful failures must endure. When you lose, take your loss and turn it into a big win for the next round you play.

The real losers try once, lose the game, and walk away complaining about how the game was rigged and that life isn't fair.

Well, guess what...**life isn't fair**. You are playing against the odds every day you wake up to face each new challenge. If you're looking for a game that is easy to win, there are plenty out there. It is called doing nothing, procrastinating, complaining, and hanging around with people who are down on the world for the way they have been treated.

Life isn't fair, and you don't deserve to win all the time. It's not what you are entitled to but that you put a target on what you want, and you want it so badly you're willing to lose 99 times before you succeed on the 100th attempt.

Life isn't meant to be a scoreboard where you tally your wins and losses. We lose a lot when risks are taken. We take risks because we want to win and gain the rewards that come with that risk.

> *"Fear of failure is the intense worry you experience when you imagine all the horrible things that could happen if you failed to achieve a goal. The intense worry increases the odds of holding back or giving up. Being successful relies to a large extent on your ability to leverage fear."*

> **— Theo Tsaousides, Ph.D**

You take a risk when you invest money. Why? To earn more money. You take a risk when you decide to get married. Why? So that you can build a life with someone, start a family, or share life's glorious adventure. You take a risk when you quit your job to start up your own company.

Why?

So that you can build your own dream instead of building someone else's. You take a risk when you get on an airplane and travel thousands of miles to a country and culture you've never been to before. Why? So that you can experience that way of life and expand your mindset.

You take a risk when you quit your full-time corporate job to pursue a career as an entrepreneur, to open your own business, and do the work you were born to do. On the one side of risk, your business could fail after five years, as 90% of them do. You could find yourself back at your corporate job with your former workers pointing at you and saying, "See, I told you so!"

This happened to me once, and it fueled my passion to dig in deeper and succeed. I was determined to not let failure be my lasting legacy, but a part of it. You have to tap into that determination, pull it up and put in front of your driving force to plow forward. When people are telling you to "Stop and be realistic", it means you're on the right path.

How far are you prepared to go?

Are you willing to risk losing your security and the possibility of being embarrassed so that you can live your life as it was meant to be lived? Will you listen to your co-workers as they go about their work, glad to have you back at your cubicle because it reinforces the truth that risk is risky. They can say, "You see, it didn't work out for Bill, so it won't work out for us either."

I have a good friend who quit his work three times before he was able to succeed in his business. When his company failed, he would go back to work to support his family and then, when he saved enough, he'd try again.

What was he risking? You could say everything. His wife was growing impatient and nervous with his persistence and not succeeding. His children were tired of telling their friends that daddy is looking for a job again. Bill's friends were concerned that he was too reckless in his attempts to succeed.

But Bill had something many people were failing to tap into: drive and determination. His ambition to succeed was stronger than his fear of failing. Was he scared of failing? Of course he was. He had a family that was relying on him for support. He had people questioning his sanity and if he should just "accept reality like the rest of us and stick with the steady 9-5."

The way Bill viewed it was that, by not succeeding, he was failing. If he gave in, like many suggested he should, the ultimate failure would be his own happiness, his soul, and the gift that he could bring to the world by making his company work.

There was risk on both sides, but while most people who judged his actions could only see it as what he stood to lose if he failed,

Bill had a different perspective. If he failed to succeed, he had everything to lose: the opportunity to create a new life, more freedom to spend with his family, and the opportunity to help people while doing what he loved to do, instead of performing mindless tasks that were handed off to him from others. For Bill, the risk was worth it.

As Robert Schuller once asked: *"What great thing would you attempt if you knew you could not fail?"*

When it comes to risk, there are two sides to every perspective. Many people see risk as dangerous. You take a chance and put your life-savings into an investment that could fail. You quit your job to start a new venture. You decide to try something new that many have never attempted before. Why do we do these things and take such chances?

For the people who are prepared to accept the risk, the fear of not succeeding is stronger than the fear of failing. It is so strong that the risk is worth it.

The Risk of Taking No Risk

Life without risk is a mediocre existence. You should take risks if the reward is great and has value. If you want something so much you can't do without it, the risk you decide to take becomes a necessary action. There are risks with an objective behind them, and then there are risks that are foolish and should be avoided.

I wouldn't race down the road in a new sports car with my seatbelt unbuckled. But I would quit my job if I wanted to pursue my dream of writing, as I recently did. Is there risk in quitting your full-time job? Of course. You might fail at your new line of work. You could run out of money or the economy crashes and you lose it all.

"And the day came when the risk to remain tight in a bud was more painful than the risk it took to blossom."

— Anais Nin

The #1 reason people stay in jobs they hate is out of fear—the fear of making a mistake, losing income, and as we already know, the fear of failing in what would otherwise be known as the great unknown.

Elon Musk, founder of Space X and PayPal and one of the greatest entrepreneurs of our time, said:

"If something is important enough you should try, even if the probable outcome is failure."

Life's full of unknowns, isn't it? How do you know you'll live to be 75? How is it that living for so long is a good thing if you've never done anything you loved?

Most people are afraid of risk. We equate risk with gambling. As any professional gambler will tell you, before you place your bet on the table, you should ask yourself, "Are you prepared to lose this money if you don't win?"

Most people are not. And we can understand that. But what is the risk you take every day when you are not taking risks to change? You are in a relationship that makes you miserable, but you are afraid to change it. Why? You might not find anyone else.

You want to quit your job and do what you love, but you are afraid to start. Why? Your job is secure and brings in a full-time paycheck, at the cost of your happiness.

I know lots of successful entrepreneurs. They all took risks to get to where they are, but they also knew the risk of not taking a risk. You risk living the rest of your life stuck, doing work you hate. You risk not leading the life you've dreamed of. You risk your mental and physical health by living in stress.

There is a story of a man who stood on the edge of an abyss. He was told that if he wanted to become the person he had always dreamed of being, he would have to step off the ledge into the darkness beneath. The man said, "But I don't know what's down there."

"Yes, that is right. Nobody does. If you did, you wouldn't jump." If you want to make a difference in your life, to change what isn't working, to tell a different story, you have to stand on that ledge and ask yourself, "Is it worth it? If I jump off and nothing catches me below, will I be okay?"

There are no guarantees. If there were, it wouldn't be a risk. And there would be no reward, either. Because reward can only be gained when you have gone through pain and work and effort to attain it.

> *"Security is mostly a superstition. Life is either a daring adventure or nothing."*
>
> **— Helen Keller**

6 Ways to Leverage Risk

(1) Let Go of Your Security

You cling to security because it feels safe. The security of a full-time job, the security of being healthy, the security of having cash in your bank…but security is a false belief in a future that is constantly changing. Your life, your health, your money, your opportunities are shifting from one day to the next.

Something could happen in an instant that throws your sense of security against the rocks and leaves you with nothing in your bank, poor health and a mountain of problems you never expected. That is the risk of living. If you're looking for a life that is perfect and without issues, a life free of risk, it doesn't exist.

(2) Seize the Day and Be Your Best

Embrace the risk of living. The next time you look at your clock on the wall, watch as the seconds tick by, and the minutes. Watch it for five minutes and then ten. You know you have a limited amount of time on this planet to do your good, play your part and create influence and deliver impact.

Don't waste this day. Seize your moment, invest in your relationships and do this one thing you were born to do. You have to be at your best every day. You must be ready. Don't let yourself fall into a life of comfortable security that doesn't exist.

Many people think life is about entitlement. Entitlement is one of the worst traps you can fall into, and it is the path to a life of failings. Success will NOT just show up because you played by all the rules. Success is the culmination of years of hard work. It is the persistent and consistent action taker that succeeds.

Life is not meant to be easy. It's easy to believe that it should be with all the false messages that surround. Don't believe in the easy path that promises to make you rich over night with minimum effort. This is a lie. If you believe in this ideology, you are setting yourself up for failure and a disappointing outcome.

The people who succeed are the people who can commit to the hard way. It means learning to live without before you can have what you want. It's about sacrificing the comfort of now and putting off your gratification.

Don't wait for someone to build you a bridge before you cross the river. If there is no river, start swimming. If there are no boats to cross the river, start swimming. If there are sharks in the water...you guessed it, start swimming. Conditions are never perfect. When the weather is stormy, that could be the best time to start your journey.

Be aware of the excuses that crop up when you're evaluating the risk. Your mind can talk you out of taking action. It taps into the fear of scarcity and directs your attention towards doing nothing.

Here are several examples of excuses you might tell yourself:

- "There will be another time, so I'll take the chance next time around."

- "If I don't succeed, people will laugh at me. I'll be too ashamed to even face anyone."

- "This has all been done before, and most people who tried, ended up failing miserably,"

- "It looks too difficult, like it could be more work than I need right now."

- "I'll wait until I have enough time. I'm too busy these days."

- "It's just not the right time. I'll wait until next year."

(3) Your Attitude Towards Risk

Henry David Thoreau said, *"What you get by achieving your goals is not as important as what you become by achieving your goals."*

It is true that when you take intentional action and do something different without knowing the outcome, there is always resistance. You feel uncomfortable. Scared. You consider backing out at the last minute.

But then a risk-taker knows the risk. They are prepared to take a loss. The risk is worth the reward. Yet, the individual that resists risk has a different mindset. They see the reward in having not failed. They are successful because they made it to the end of the day without losing anything. They feel safe and secure in the false belief that risk is an unnecessary action to take.

So, why do we not take more chances? The excuses we use are overpowering. Here are just a few of the bad thoughts that hold you back from taking that leap:

- The risk of loss is too great.

- The comparison trap: "I've seen people fail at this before…"

- Regret: "If I fail, I'll live to regret it…"

- Motivation: "I'll do it when I feel motivated. And right now, I don't…"

- Excuses: "It is a lot of work and I'm too busy…"

- Procrastination: "I'll wait until I'm ready…"

(4) The Way Forward is Always Up

Most risks people take might appear to be foolish to others. They might even try to talk you out of it, reminding you of the dangers involved and what will happen to you if it doesn't work out. But risk is largely based on perspective as well.

Your risks have to be smart. The risk you are taking must be worth the reward. What do you have to gain by taking this chance? Is there value in the risk that prompts you to move ahead?

If you try something bold, you could fail. You might lose your savings, your time, or your confidence. But these things are not the be-all and end-all. What you stand to lose by not taking intentional action is far greater. You risk losing your dream. You risk living the rest of your life always wondering, "If only I had…". The risk of living with regret is far greater than any risk of losing material wealth.

You always risk failure, not because of what you tried and failed at, but because of what you didn't try in the first place. Herein lies the real failure in life. How many people die with their music still playing in their souls? How many meet the end of their days knowing they have no more second chances in life? Will you be one of these people who make excuses until the end, afraid to do that one thing you've always dreamed of but never took the first step?

Your life is at risk every moment of the day. It could all end today. And if it does, you want to be there, ready to say that you did everything in this life to make it the best you can. You want to be able to say that failure never held you back, and even when you were scared, in those moments of fear and doubt and uncertainty, you ignored the fear and made it happen anyway.

(5) Failing Fast in Motion

Do you have goals for this year? Do you know what they are? If you do, I want you to pull out your goals and read them over.

How do you feel about your goals? Scared, possible, maybe doable? Or do you feel nothing, and it wouldn't matter one way or the other if you achieved them? Most people, when they set goals (and 90% of the population do not), they set targets that are either too easy to hit or too vague to be seen. Make your goal a risk. Take one goal this year and challenge yourself to achieve it.

Your goal could be to achieve $50,000 in sales for your company. Well, increase that to $500,000. How can you achieve this? I don't know, I'm not you. But what I do know is, life will always deliver what you ask of it.

In a poem written by J.B. Rittenhouse, titled "My Wage", the last sentence is enough to make you stop, think, and question everything you ask for. It says: *"I worked for a menial's hire, only to learn dismayed, that any wage I had asked of life, life would have surely paid."*

You always get what you ask for, and never more than that. You could get less than you ask for, but as soon as you set the limit on your wage, that's your price and you'll get no more.

When it comes to the goal challenge, take a risk. Be bold. Go with courage and set a goal for yourself that seems absolutely ridiculous. You're not the first person to do this. People are making dreams happen, not by chance or some lucky wager, but intentional action driven by a goal that must be seen to the end.

You don't have to be Bill Gates to take a risk. You just have to know what you want, and then find a way to get it. It's time to raise the stakes. You can only fail big if you live large.

(6) The Risk of Saying "NO"

Everything you are saying NO to could be what is making you stuck. Are you saying NO to an opportunity because there are risks involved? If so, how much do you stand to gain if you win? How much could you lose if you try and fail? How much could you lose if you do nothing and fail anyway?

Right now, make a list of what you say NO to every day. Here is what my list looks like:

- No, I won't work out today. I'd rather watch TV and put on more weight.

- No, I won't work on my new business. I'd rather go to work for someone else and stay miserable, doing work that I hate.

- No, I won't change my thoughts. I'd rather hold onto my old way of thinking that makes me unhappy.

- No, I won't leave this relationship. I'd rather stay with this person and waste my time trying to make them happy.

We avoid taking risks, no matter how small, because we want to keep what we have. "I'll do it someday when I'm ready," you say. "I'll do it when I have enough time, enough resources, or enough confidence."

But the day you wish for never arrives. Life doesn't care about what you do or think or decide. It will continue to move forward regardless of your choices. Years will go by and you get older but are still holding onto that same frame of mind.

Still wishing for that perfect day when it will all be in your favor. I can tell you this: the only day that matters and the only time you have is now. So, are you ready to take this day and do something great with it? Can you visualize where you will be six months from now if you make a change?

Change should never be something that happens to you. It is not an event, or a play put on by someone else. You are the stage director, and the prop manager, and the producer of your own show. In other words, the world is an audience and you are here to put on the greatest show anyone has ever seen.

Here is a quote by the Former Associate Justice of the Supreme Court of the United States, Oliver Wendell Holmes Sr.:

"Many people die with their music still in them. Too often it is because they are always getting ready to live. Before they know it, time runs out."

Are you ready to play your music so the world can enjoy your creativity? Or will you wait for that perfect day when it feels right? Procrastination is a game the mind plays when it struggles against mental obstacles. Your obstacle is you.

But as Ryan Holiday has written in *The Obstacle is the Way*: "*If it is the way, you have to charge through it and accept it as the only path worth taking.*"

Eight Ways Failure Influences Success

> *"Failure should be our teacher, not our undertaker. Failure is delay, not defeat. It is a temporary detour, not a dead end. Failure is something we can avoid only by saying nothing, doing nothing, and being nothing."*
>
> **— Denis Waitley**

Failing is a dynamic learning curve. The ability to fail and maintain a positive attitude throughout the process is a hallmark of every successful achiever.

For many, failure can mean the end of the road. If you lose your business, you never start up a new one. If you fail in a relationship, you give up on dating to avoid rejection. If your book gets rejected by several publishers, you throw it in the trash and never write again.

Failure impacts us all in unique and different ways. It has strong influence over your decisions, the action you take, and the outcome of your goals. Failure can lead to deep feelings of inadequacy, shame, and the fear of rejection. You question your commitment to push forward and try again. Many people get stuck, lost in uncertainty, become demotivated and trapped in a sea of negative thinking.

As you spiral down into self-doubt and question your WHY, you find yourself on the ropes, fighting hard in the last round of your life before hitting the mat.

As you move through this book, I want you to think about your emotional attachment to failure. Ask questions when you stumble against challenges and get honest with yourself. How does failing impact your confidence? What stream of thoughts take over your mind? Do you look for excuses to give up and do something less risky?

One reason you struggle with failure and allow it to impact your mind in a negative way can be traced back to conditioning. Some people fail and continue to charge forward, no matter the setback. Two people can fail at the same goal and yet, one will carry on, and the other person gives up.

What is the difference? When you survive failure, and decide to carry on, you gain experience and knowledge. You build up a thick skin called *perseverance*. While most people shrink back to assess and question if moving ahead and trying again is worth it, when you master the fear of failing, you lose the grip of fear that holds you back.

One of my earlier mentors had a saying: Take action now. Take your failures as lessons. Move forward.

My mentor was an action taker. He failed a lot. He didn't care either. As a result, he ended up becoming very successful in his business while others were losing their shirts and then crying about it in a drink at the local bar. One day, we met up for coffee and he said to me, "I just found out that my business lost $20k. One of the employees I trusted was stealing from me, and he's disappeared. The money is gone, too."

I remember thinking at the time he was going to go bankrupt or close the business. Instead he said, "I guess I'll have to screen applicants more closely." And that was it. He tightened up his hiring policy, trained his employees to perform at a productive rate faster than anybody else, and within 18 months had earned back the money lost plus, his business was thriving again.

Failure comes at a cost, but it doesn't have to cost you everything. Most lessons in life are free if you pay attention and learn from failure. If you want to succeed, watch how successful people make a comeback after taking a dive. How do they react? What is the first decision they make? Do they panic out of fear and shut everything down like turtles ducking into a shell? No.

Failure impacts your rate of success. But how it influences you comes down to your attitude towards the situation.

Here are eight ways that failure influences your life and leads to a successful outcome of your goals. Stay fixed on your behavior and how you react when faced with a difficult situation. Tap into your growth mindset and step out of the comfort zone. Let yourself be scared…and take intentional action anyway.

(1) Failure Conditions You to Take More.

Conditioning your mind and attitude to fail is preparing yourself for success. You can't succeed unless you fail forward to get there. Anyone who tells you, "Oh yeah, I made it this far and never failed once," is implying three truths:

1. They haven't tried hard enough to succeed

2. They are taking the wrong kind of action

3. They are accepting the lowest denominator of gains and calling it success without trial. The more you are conditioned to fail, the easier it will become.

Boxers train their bodies for years to take hard punches. Professional skiers fall down hundreds of times on the slopes before making it to the bottom with a near-perfect score. Artists and creatives produce bad work before it is considered a masterpiece. The more you practice and put in the time and work, the less you fail and, your fails lead to mastery.

You cannot fake experience. You need to put yourself in a situation that invites discomfort. Jumping out of your comfort zone, stepping onto center stage in the middle of severe stage fright, and refusing to be beaten when you've just lost for the 20th time.

Focus on conditioning your mindset. When you come against resistance, identify the action you're resisting. That is an obvious pain point. Your goal is to break this resistance when it gets in your way. Force your mind to push back hard. Don't allow excuses to divert your focus. The more you fight, the easier winning will become. Within a few months, the obstacles that once challenged you will be broken.

(2) Failing is Your Greatest Teacher.

If you fail, are you a failure? There is only one way to be a true failure—when you give up on your dream halfway and go back to failing at the life you hate.

When you settle for what life gives you, instead of what you create from your life, failure is your result. You fail yourself when you settle for what is available. But failing in and of itself is what gives you courage: the courage to push on, to say NO, to develop a belief in your strengths.

If you see your mistakes and hardships as a necessary path, instead of an obstacle that keeps you stuck, you can tap into your internal strength to break any challenge. You have to form a concrete perspective of, not just who you are now but, who you intend to become.

Henry David Thoreau once said:

"What you get by achieving your goals is not as important as what you become by achieving your goals."

What is the vision you're creating for yourself? How will others who look up to you perceive you? Do you want your friends, family, and children to be inspired by your commitment to striving for greatness?

If yes, you have to act with greatness. Self-doubt and uncertainly will always challenge you when you step out of your comfort zone. But you decide if you will buy into the lies:

"I failed so I am worthless."

"I failed so that means everything is doomed to fail."

The lies are never-ending, until you put an end to them. Turn off the negative internal voices. Tune into your voice of positive encouragement. It is the voice that speaks to you with confidence, love, and assurance.

Everyone fears failing until they fail and survive. We build up a negative view of what it means to fail. You perceive it as something you won't survive, or "this is the end of everything" if you don't make it. I've failed many times over, and I was always scared of it. But I always came through on the other side. I had a few scars from the course of battle with the challenges I faced, but defeat was never an option.

As Benjamin Franklyn said: *"The things which hurt, instruct."*

You can perceive failure as your greatest teacher. As you open your mind to the instruction it has to teach you, your life becomes a lesson in personal mastery. This is an education you cannot learn in school.

Let failure be your guide. Appreciate your mistakes moving forward and take comfort in knowing you are growing stronger, developing resiliency, and be grateful for the opportunity to be on a path of constant and never-ending improvement.

(3) Failure Shifts Your Attitude Towards Desiring Change.

If there is one thing failing can teach you it is this: Change is necessary to make progress. If you are not trying new things, attempting and failing at them, your character growth stagnates. You drop into a rut. Change comes with crushing your obstacles and deciding to keep going.

Your life is about experiencing as much failure as you can. Kids make more mistakes than anyone, until adults teach them mistakes are not cool and they must be careful. But being careful can invite fear into your life too.

You start being cautious; then you start to fear what will happen if you screw up. And as you start to avoid taking risk, you also avoid changing the way things are. Change can only happen when you do something different.

(4) Failure Tests Your Commitment

Fail once and you try again. Fail twice and ... what would you do? Let's take Thomas Edison as an example. We all know how resilient he was and how, despite failure after failure, he kept trying. Walt Disney failed repeatedly for years and he kept going. So, this tells us something about failure: It tests your level of commitment.

If you're working for something you believe in, and you are determined to get it no matter the cost, failing as you go is a testament to how committed you are. People who give up just short of the finish line or stop trying after falling down a few times don't have the commitment to finish. They get passed over by the few determined enough to take it to the end of the finish line.

(5) Failure Influences Your Rate of Growth

People who avoid mistakes because they might fail are setting themselves up for failure right away. By avoiding potential mistakes, you are also giving up on taking the right actions leading to important lessons learned.

Most of our lessons in life can be taken from mistakes made. Maybe you had to make the same mistake several times before you got it right. Your rate of growth and how you learn is immediately connected with your ability to try.

Many people don't even try. They wait for the perfect moment when they have enough courage, or enough money, or the time is right. But the moment is never perfect and one day to the next life is in motion and moving things around. You have to take action no matter the circumstances.

Failing is not the setback we think it is. Just the opposite. People who make lots of mistakes and fail fast are on an accelerated learning curve. They are failing at a fast rate because they jump right in and go for it. If you accept failing as your only way to learn, you pull back on hesitation and accept the outcome no matter what it is.

(6) Failure Influences the People You Bring into Your Life

By overcoming and persevering through failure, you level up your mindset and shift to a new role in the game. True failures, people who fail by default in life for not taking action, never change and invariably seek out like-minded people who think and act just like they do. If you are set on winning and you refuse to accept failing as your end game, you want to connect with the people on that same wave length.

If you are hanging with people who are not interested in growth or expanding past their zone of comfort, they will drag you down with them. No matter how strong you are, eventually you will fall. Failure influences your choice as to whom you spend valuable time with.

If time is your greatest resource and it is limited (and we know it is) then it is critical you seek out high-end influencers that are determined to help you rise up and be the best you can be. Hell, you want to be better than you were the day before.

(7) Failure Influences Your Sense of Self-Worth

By failing, and seeing the worst of your failure through, you gain a greater sense of worth. You become fail-worthy by proving to your own mind that everything you believed about failure has been wrong from the beginning.

One of the greatest realizations I had years ago was coming to realize that my old way of thinking had me believing failure devalued your worth and made you a less-than person. Failure means you are worthless in the eyes of everyone. But, in fact, it is your self-worth that increases when you charge through hard times and make it work no matter what.

This is character building at its best; when you are willing to put your character out there, to challenge the way of thinking of the many and take destiny into your own hands. Failure influences your sense of self-worth because it increases your personal value built on your ability to break through resistance with grit and resiliency.

Your level of self-worth is in tandem with your willingness to fail, to do whatever it takes to succeed, to challenge events, people and even principles and rules when everything is going against you and say, "No." If you believe in what you are doing, and you believe in your mission, you do not need permission to act.

(8) Failure Influences Your Habits

The habits you feed are the habits that determine your rate of overcoming failure. Let's take a look. If you want to lose weight but so far have failed to do so, are your habits concurrent with someone who wants to lose weight? If you are feeding into a system of bad habits, you will fail to get the results you truly want. Your system of habits plays a major role in how you fail.

With a system of good habits that are pushing you to grow, you can fail and continue to make progress. But bad habits will always fail you and hold you back, driving your rate of failure into the negative. The approach is simple, but execution is the challenge. It is one thing to say, "I am going to stop eating junk food for 30 days so that I can lose weight." You have the intention but following through requires another level of effort.

Your good habits will always fuel your success, even when you slip out of habit. Bad habits are anything detrimental to your true desire. If you want to improve your health but you're still smoking, obviously you're going to fail to feel great about yourself. Shift away from this habit and replace it with 30–60 minutes of cardio performed 3-5 times per week.

Failure in other areas of your life can influence your habits. If you experience failure in your business or personal relationships, you might try to drown out reality by binging on sugar or alcohol. Stress and anxiety brought on by worry, self-esteem issues or both can bring out the worst in your habits.

I strongly suggest you spend 30 minutes of quiet reflection time a day. This could be spent taking a walk or in meditation. Building a system of good habits into your morning and daily routine will avert the potential failure that bad habits bring.

Defeat Your
Failure Disappointment

Failure can be a crippling, disappointing experience for most people. You came 2nd place in a marathon when you were expected to be placed first. You missed passing a test by 2%. You failed to land your dream job because another interviewee went to a better university. The person you finally decided to ask out on a date said no. The business you invested all of your savings in failed after the first year.

These kinds of near-misses and failures can damage self-esteem, create feelings of hopelessness, and make you feel worthless. This sets you up for further failure expectations later.

The next race you enter, you are less confident; the next job interview you go to, you show up with a failing posture, looking as if you have no hope in hell of getting that job either. You have strong resistance to asking someone out on a date because you're expecting another rejection. Feeling less competent, less motivated, and less of everything else, you start slipping back into repetitive thoughts that destroy your positive mindset.

What you are experiencing is disappointment on a larger scale. This is a deep disappointment in yourself. You not only let others down, but you failed yourself. You start to doubt that any actions moving forward will amount to nothing but more failure, more people rejecting you, and more loss. This way of thinking is distorted and damages your self-esteem and feelings of self-worth.

You begin the pain train of negative putdowns:

- "I'm no good."

- "I can't believe I thought that I had a chance. What was I thinking?"

- "This is the last time I take this kind of risk."

- "Only losers come in 2nd place."

- "If only I were smarter, wiser, better looking…"

- "I never stood a chance anyway."

This psychological warfare with yourself can only end one way: **your giving up and accepting failure as the final outcome**. Your refusing to try again for fear of losing. The ego plays a large role in this story. The ego hates to lose because it has convinced you how unstoppable, unbeatable, and how great you are.

The psychological power of failure can be damaging, but that doesn't mean you have to accept it. All of us are disappointed when we fail at something. You're not supposed to like it, but what you can do is combat against the feelings of helplessness, hopelessness and despair.

That feeling of deep disappointment in yourself is natural. You expect to succeed when you prepared hard for the interview, studied many late nights for that test, or trained every day on the field for the race.

But failing in and of itself is not the final conclusion. It is only final if you decide that you are done, you give up, never to pursue any more challenges ever again. But this is what failure really is: giving up when you are so close to succeeding the next time around. Throwing in the towel when all you had to do is push a little harder, make another attempt, and increase your skillset to give yourself the best chance at success.

Making that critical decision to never try again so you don't have to go through the emotional suffering of feeling like a failure leads to a pattern of self-defeat. Failure can impact our self-esteem and conjure up false conclusions about our character. To make it worse, if you surround yourself with a crowd that is unsupportive, they remind you of your failure through putdowns:

- "You see, told you it wouldn't work."

- What were you thinking, that you were better than us?"

- "Don't worry, nobody ever succeeds at that. You're no different."

In attempting to overcome this disappointment in yourself, you look for ways to avoid embarrassment, humiliation, and shame. You set your expectations low, reduce your expected performance level, and generate excuses for why you shouldn't try as hard from now on. You might feel 'exhausted' or that you need a break before taking on another challenge.

Be careful with this approach. Your reasoning could be your way of secretly escaping. You unconsciously lower your expectations and put off responding or taking immediate action. The fear of failing—and the disappointment that it incurs—strikes you so deeply that you're intimidated to try again. This intimidation leads to fear, and your fear takes you into depression and feeling like an absolute failure at everything.

Let's not go there. Before you make that decision to give up, create a list of options. If giving up isn't an option, what is the action step you can take right now to move yourself ahead just one step.

You must ask yourself: *What's my next move?* I'm disappointed that I didn't succeed, so I have one of two paths I can take here:

1. I give up and go back to my life as it was before this. I stop pursuing all goals, stop taking risks, and eliminate any activity that could potentially lead to my disappointing failure again.

2. I suck it up and try again. Only I train harder, look better, work faster…and if I fail again, I try harder the next time.

You decide the path it takes to overcome personal disappointment. So, here it is. You can prepare yourself for winning by focusing on doing your best. Train hard, practice hard, work hard. Then, when you do miss the goal and end up in 2nd or even 10th place, you know you did your best at that time. The only position that is worse than last place in a race is giving up. Winners finish the race regardless of where they are at.

> *"Pearls don't lie on the seashore. If you want one, you must dive for it."*
>
> ## — Chinese proverb

There are no limits on how good you can become. And there will always be competitors training harder than you. But don't resent or envy your competition. Learn from the people who are better than you, who beat you, and use the tactics they applied to get as good as they are.

Learn from your competition. But find a way to do it better. Find out what works for you and keep scaling up your efforts. The only time you should be disappointed is, not if you fail but, when you don't train hard enough to win.

Turn off the negative badgering when it begins in your mind. It's the negative monster in your head that is your worst enemy, and not anybody else. Another person cannot put a negative thought in your mind, no matter what you tell yourself. Filter out the garbage running through your mind and stay focused on your moment.

By believing in those negative thoughts, you make yourself a helpless victim. You validate all the reasons why you should quit. Your internal disappointment takes over your mind by feeding into negative messages that are not true.

As Leonard Mlodinow said: *"A failure doesn't mean you are unworthy, nor does it preclude success on the next try."*

There is no guarantee of success, even when you do your best. You will still fail on your good days. But you can be guaranteed failure if you choose not to act. You will fail if you buy into negative self-talk. You will fail indefinitely if you let disappointment linger and lead you into a darker place.

Moving forward, you will train yourself to take a positive approach towards failure. From this moment on, you will see failing as a necessary stage for winning. Win big or fail big, it's all the same when you play at your best and let excellence carve the to the finish line.

Eliminate Failure Disappointment with 3 Strategies

Here are 3 steps you can take to eliminate disappointment when you fail:

(1). Kill Your Inaccurate Generalizations.

The negative messages that creep in after you experience a letdown are loaded to tear you apart. These are the voices that lead to feelings of shame and humiliation. Remember, your internal voice isn't a separate entity. It's your mind reacting to stress, worry and fear. It responds by default in warning you of the risks that are involved.

In trying to find reasons for why you failed to succeed, it delivers images of why you are not meant to have it all. You make trips to the past and validate your present failure with previous failures. Failure can be very convincing. First, it knocks you down, and then it hits you when you're down. All your preconceived notions about failing are grounded in fears and lies swimming in your mind.

Self-criticism can do as much damage as someone else criticizing you. When you have a setback, you immediately drum up all the reasons it happened. These reasons turn into beliefs, and beliefs become limitations grounded in fear. In this case, when you generalize about why you aren't good enough, what went wrong, or how other people are much better than you are, you might hesitate to try anything new.

You can change your mind about what failure means to you. You can determine if it is a detriment to your progress, or a part of it. You will discover that, by ridding your mind of false accusations, it opens the way for honest, natural communication with your true self.

Breathe deeply and relax your mind and body. Take the pressure away from always having to be active and charging ahead. Step back, stop, re-evaluate where you're at, and plan your next move.

There are times when our goals seem hopelessly out of reach. But day by day, year by year, you get closer. You succeed, not through big wins where heavy risk is involved, but the smaller steps that lead to smaller wins that lead to greater gains in the long-term.

(2). Fail Now, Succeed Later

I've said that failure is inevitable. And it really is. One perspective that works is to know right up front you're not going to win on your first try. You probably won't win on your second attempt, either.

You might have twenty attempts at landing a good job and fail to get any of them. Or the first one hundred sales calls you made this morning resulted in zero leads and no sales. The first five books you wrote and published made you less money than minimum wage at a convenience store. The first three business ventures you launched all failed within a year. Your first marriage failed after five years.

But what does all of this mean? Do we stop trying?

When I was discussing this with my mentor, he said: "You can fail now, or fail later. I know many people who have procrastinated for years on goals and dreams they talked about. The underlying fear is that they would fail at the one thing that mattered most to them. But to do what you love requires a persistence built only through making those first mistakes. Waiting for the time to be right won't change the rules around this."

Fail Now or fail later.

Fear holds us back and we think, "I'll do this when I'm feeling more confident" or "I'll try again someday when the time is right."

You can fail now or later, only, the latter becomes more difficult. If it takes ten years for you to succeed, you need to try, test it, and fail for the first five years. At year ten, you gain positive reinforcement from accumulating victories.

If you are holding onto a dream that is brewing inside of you, now is the time to start. You might not have the chance to "fail later." There will never be a perfect moment. Now is the time to fail.

As Zig Ziglar said, *"You don't have to be great to start, but you do have to start to be great."*

Start today.

Fail now.

Succeed Later.

(3) Pursuing Your Life Mission IS the Journey.

We talk about achieving a goal, becoming #1, and succeeding as if it is the end result that brings happiness. But isn't it the small wins and failures along the way? After you reach a goal, aren't you soon preparing for the next one?

The psychology of failure teaches you that, not only is failing to be expected but, failing your way on the journey is the journey. If you meet anyone that succeeded and is living their dream, the question they get asked the most is: "How did you do it?"

Listen to their story and you'll hear a tale of overcoming obstacles, constant attempts that failed in the beginning, and a long journey of wins and losses until they made it.

And after you make it, life doesn't end there. You keep going, pushing to the next level, taking your next challenge.

If you are frustrated by lack of progress and you want things to move faster, you are trying to rid your mind of the disappointment it's holding onto from not having succeeded. Your success is today, by showing up and giving it your all. It is the pursuit that makes the story worthwhile. If it takes you twenty years to make it, then that is going to be a great story when you're ready to tell it.

Always remember the journey and your steps along the way. Making steady progress, learning lessons and new tactics, meeting new people and forging quality relationships is the best success anyone can hope for.

Destroy Your Fearful Excuses

> *"There is no failure except in no longer trying. There is no defeat except from within, no really insurmountable barrier save our own inherent weakness of purpose."*
>
> **— Frank McKinney**

Excuses are false justifications created to convince us why we can't live the way we want to. This is a powerful form of self-deception—a lie within a lie that keeps us trapped. Excuses that support our failures are based on a foundation of false beliefs.

Nothing is possible when you are afraid to try new things or explore possibilities. This level of fear is intended to destroy your potential for growth and development.

Created through multiple fears—the fear of failure, the fear of rejection, the fear of success, or the fear of change—in buying into excuses, you allow negative thought patterns to take control of your mind. This impacts the direction of your life.

In believing all the reasons you can't or shouldn't take action, you are held back by the fears of "What if...?"

For example:

- "What if I fail?"

- "What if it doesn't work out like I want it to?"

- "What if I lose all my money?"

- "What if nobody likes me?"

- "What if I make a fool out of myself?"

There is a way to overcome these self-defeating thoughts. By talking back with confidence and taking intentional action against your internal voices of fear and uncertainty, fearful excuses lose all power of reasoning.

Once you stop creating excuses for why you can't, you form a new attitude and develop a positive way of thinking. With a shift in perspective, you create a system of new habits and thought patterns, leading to intentional choice.

When you develop the habit of thinking positively and turning every negative situation into a chance to heal, negative excuses no longer have support to control your thoughts or actions. You are free to make better choices leading toward a successful outcome instead of repetitive failure.

The Gift of Iron Will

Regardless of your profession, wealth or social status, failings happen to everyone. Failing is one of the prime necessities for self-development and growth. When you fail repeatedly to achieve your goal or accomplish your dreams in life, it hurts. You build resentment. You want to make it but the distance from here to there is so far, it feels a thousand miles away.

Think about what **Winston Churchill** said about failure:

> *"Success consists of going from failure to failure without loss of enthusiasm."*

Failure makes you better. It is the grit that drives you to excel at whatever it is you're striving for. When disappointment creeps into your mind, kick it out of there. When fear takes over and you feel yourself folding, tell yourself, "I'm feeling the fear but I'm doing it anyway." If someone suggests you give up because it is too difficult, you recall the hundreds of successful men and women who fought through adversity.

You recognize these failures:

- Michael Jordan missed most of the shots he ever took.

- J.K. Rowling's mega-bestseller *Harry Potter and the Sorcerer's Stone* was rejected by multiple agents.

- Walt Disney was fired from the Kansas City Star for lack of imagination.

- Bill Gates' first business failed.

- Colonel Sanders' fried chicken recipe was rejected by over 1000 restaurants when he was at the age of 65 and living on a $105 a month social security check.

- Jack Canfield's book *Chicken Soup for the Soul* was rejected 144 times, and he was laughed at by a publisher when Canfield told him the book was going to sell half a million copies.

Failure is everywhere. Excuses are everywhere, too. It's up to you if you believe in your fears or master your courage.

The more chances you take to try different things, the more you increase the risk of failing. The only people I know of who never make mistakes or fail at something are those who never try anything different. They don't accept new challenges or have the desire to be challenged in any way. They stay stuck, not because they can't take intentional action, but by deciding they won't. They fall into the same routine day after day and take as few risks as possible to avoid stumbling and looking foolish.

If you fall into this trap, you reduce your risk of failing, but you also fail to break through your own limitations. You create a comfort zone that turns into a prison and reduces your chances of achieving the level of success you could have.

Many of your failures might have left you with painful memories: relationships that never made it, bad investments, dead-end jobs, stage failure, or embarrassing moments that left you traumatized. It is so painful that you decided to never do that again. But in making that decision, you are also choosing to fail by default.

By not getting back up and trying again, you accept failing as the final outcome. This is when growth ends. When you stop growing and leveling up, you don't just stay stuck. You fall back and regress. You fear looking bad.

It doesn't have to be this way. You have more strength than you know. The mind is not always right. When in the midst of failure, it makes you question everything, right down to who you are and why you're here. But failure, as painful as it can be, is a necessary part of life. It's the pathway to your dreams and goals. Failure is not just part of the journey, it is the journey.

Walt Disney said, *"All our dreams can come true, if we have the courage to pursue them."*

Whatever we desire is within the realm of possibility, but your negative thinking supports the self-doubt that drives away chances of success. Negative thoughts create beliefs like, "I can't do it," or "I'm not cut out for that," or "Someone else will come up with a better idea." You have to eliminate this pattern of destructive thinking before it has time to complete its cycle of self-defeat.

No matter the obstacle, you will face your darkest hour and persevere. It is this iron will that cuts through the fear and breaks all obstacles—the willingness to do whatever it takes to achieve a vision, to accomplish a magnificent goal, and to do everything you can to overcome self-defeat.

Read this statement and commit it to memory:

People who succeed in spite of failures are made of an iron will that few others possess. They keep trying. When one path doesn't work, they try another. With every failure, they succeed because they are getting closer to achieving their goals.

Excuses: Pathways to Failure

Forming excuses is a method used to avoid the fear of taking a risk. Instead of just going for it, people are too afraid to risk looking stupid or damaging their egos through embarrassment. We would rather take the easy way out and make excuses for all the reasons why taking action isn't an option.

The justifications created that force you to submit to passive inactivity are more damaging than the worst failures you could endure. The definition of a true failure isn't someone who tried and never succeeded, but rather someone who never had the courage to try in the first place.

By failing to act, you produce the same results as if you had tried and failed. So, wouldn't it be better to just give it a shot? Would you rather take a chance and see what happens? Ask yourself, "What is the worst thing that could happen?" If you can accept the worst-case scenario, you've nothing to lose.

Failing to pursue the things you want in life is a failure in disguise. We use excuses to defend ourselves from the hurts of the world as we build walls that protect limited interests and fragile egos, and to preserve the limited field of vision through which we view the world. Your excuses for not pursuing your dreams might appear to be valid, but under the surface is a path that leads to false reasoning and bitter defeat.

Here are some more excuses we use to convince ourselves not to take a risk:

- "I am too old for that."

- "It didn't work for my friends, so why should it work for me?"

- "I'll wait until someone else does it and succeeds."

- "I'm too busy right now. When things calm down, I'll…"

- "I don't have the right skill set."

- "I'm still outlining the BIG plan."

- "That's just not who I am."

- "The initial investment is just too much. I can't afford to lose that money."

- "I've been working at this job for twenty years, so it's too late to change now."

When you make excuses for not taking immediate action, it strengthens your determination to follow the path of least resistance. The ego uses excuses to control your situation, whether you love it or hate it. A day will come when someone else will take the risk that you didn't, and they will succeed where you failed.

Their ultimate success will become your tragic failure. Their gain becomes your loss. They might stumble a few times before getting it right, but they will eventually get it, and prosper from the success you could have had.

"Fear: False Evidence Appearing Real."

If you want to avoid this, the key is to not think about what you have to lose if you fail. Ask yourself: *what will I gain if I succeed?*

This shift in perception is powerful. One train of thought keeps you stuck in scarcity (I might lose what I have) and the other way of thinking focuses on abundance (I'll gain so much if I succeed).

When it appears difficult to achieve your goal, write down the one thing that you've always wanted that this course of action could deliver to you. Don't give yourself permission to fail through fear. Many people give up just short of the finish line, and they have no idea how close they were to making it.

Use Visualization to Burn Your Excuses

Visualization is a powerful exercise. Most people underestimate the energy created by repeatedly visualizing their 'future success'. Focus on this vision when you stumble and don't succeed the first time. Constantly run this vision through your mind, over and over again. Visualize yourself living this dream.

Robert Collier said, *"Visualize this thing that you want, see it, feel it, believe in it. Make your mental blue print and begin to build."*

Excuses, fear, or negative thoughts have no defense against a powerful vision. It sharpens focus and funnels all your energy into a single stream of concentrated effort. Creating this mental snapshot of where you are now and where you want to be is incredibly powerful.

By integrating the tool of visualization in your daily habits, you develop the capability to become rich in every way. You are the visual architect supplying the plans and blueprints. You bring your ideas to the table; the visual imagination is the carpenter of your dreams.

You can implement the practice of visualization into your daily routine. Start by asking yourself these questions:

- What would you do if there were no limitations to the kind of life you desire?
- How would you spend the rest of your days if your excuses couldn't stop you from pushing forward?
- What would it take for you to accomplish everything you have ever dreamed possible?
- What opportunities do you wish you had? How will you create these opportunities?
- What event do you envision that will have a profound impact on your life?
- What is the life you visualize living someday?
- What actions could you take every day to bring you closer to achieving this dream?

"I think to visualize failure as you're starting off is really a bad thing to do."

— Marcia Gay Harden

Talk Back to Your Excuses

The key to facing your personal fears is to take away the power of negative ideas and concepts by removing any unhealthy thoughts that have constructed a false reality. Talk back to your excuses.

These excuses are the same ones you've been using for years to keep the lies real. To avoid facing challenges and grasping opportunities, we create excuses as to why we can't. This behavior of negative self-talk can be diverted with practice, eventually removed, and replaced with more positive, high-powered images of yourself taking on more proactive roles.

Too many people have grown old and realized they could have been more and done more, but fear held them back. Now the fear is a different kind—the fear of knowing they will never have the chance to do the things they always wanted to do.

Make it a habit to avoid making excuses. Do not accept anything as being impossible to obtain until you've exhausted every known effort to succeed.

Create enough positive reasons as to why you should do it. If you find yourself making up multiple reasons for why you can't, step back and analyze how you feel at that moment. In many cases, these negative feelings influence the justifications we create.

You can change your excuses from words of weakness to words of power that inspire and encourage you to overcome your fears.

Regret Before Dying

Bonnie Ware was a nurse who worked in palliative care for many years. Her patients were people who went home to die. Bonnie spent time with each one before they passed away. She asked them to share regrets they had during their lives. Common themes emerged from the interviews. This was the core message many had in common:

> *I wish I'd had the courage to live a life true to myself, not the life others expected of me.*

When you reach the end of your life, will you look back without regret? If you have regrets, what are they? Is it too late to change these events?

The past cannot change, but we can make a difference today. What dreams have you been putting off? Are you still waiting for happiness instead of creating it for yourself?

Regardless of your age, it is never too late to do what you've always wanted to do. Remember you have the power to reinvent who you are at any given time. You can make priority decisions to live in a way that expresses fully who you are as an individual.

The terminal patients interviewed by Bonnie Ware held deep regrets for things they never did and fears that held them back. By failing to make choices that can change your destiny, you are setting yourself up for regret. Instead, choose to become your absolute best.

Your dreams are too important to fall victim to excuses. Start converting excuses into positive words of empowerment. You are not powerless; you wield great power from within.

The Power of Choice

What's important is not whether you lose or fail—it's what you do *after* you fail that matters. Will you make an excuse to avoid trying it again? Will you take the easy and safe path, treading lightly without any risk of stumbling? Or will you embrace your greatest moment of defeat and turn it into a victory? Are you willing to rise up to meet the next challenge?

There is a choice to make. Embrace your failures and look for the chance to turn a loss into a win. We are educated to think that losing is all about failing and failing is bad. But it's not. When we stumble and nothing works out the way it should have, it isn't the end of the world.

You can bounce back, get up again, and give it another shot. Most things you are afraid to fail at are really golden opportunities in disguise. You can choose to ignore these opportunities or take a chance and act on them.

If you listen to your fear and react to it by staying passive, you will be paralyzed indefinitely, unable to think or take action. Your fears will win and you will be defeated at every turn. You must be willing to rise up again after experiencing those continuous knockdowns, and to refuse to give in when the odds are stacked against you.

A mentor of mine had a saying: "Always be the last man standing." In a race, after everyone else has given up, you are the one still trying to reach the finish line. When the market turns bad and you just suffered a financial hit, you'll be looking for ways to make more money. When people say that what you are chasing is impossible, become a believer in the impossible. This is the attitude that champions adopt.

You can create a motivating positive force by pushing forward, working with your fear and using it as leverage. It's like molding clay. Until you pick it up and start working with it, it remains in its original state. You have the power of choice to create whatever you desire, regardless of present conditions.

Take Charge and Make a Choice

You can start today by taking charge and accepting full responsibility for your life. Live the empowered lifestyle you know you want.

As you learn to talk back to negative messages, you will experience change. Stop convincing yourself why you can't and tell yourself why you can, and the reasons why you feel you deserve this— because you do!

Our excuses are convincing, but they won't stand a chance against the counterattack of a positive statement. For a long time, I used to say to myself, "Why me? Why would anyone want to hire me? Why should someone want to pay me for my work when there's always someone out there who can do it better? Who is going to believe in me when I can't even believe in myself? What do I have to offer?"

I realized these questions were negative and could only lead deeper into thinking like a failure. I took a different approach and started asking, "Hey, why not me?" When you find yourself making a negative excuse, identify the source and replace it with the opposite.

Take a look at the following examples:

I will get to it someday.

Get started on your dream today. If you wait for someday, you will never do it. All your excuses are running out with each new day. It is today that presents the greatest opportunity. Will you seize it, or will you wait for 'someday' that may never arrive?

I lack the discipline to succeed.

Nobody lacks discipline. We lack worthy goals that motivate and inspire us to take immediate action. If you think you have no discipline, it is because you have goals that don't motivate you or get you excited enough to do anything about them.

Write down your goals as soon as possible and get to work on them. Discipline is not something you are born with. It is a practice you work at to become proficient. Start disciplining your words and thoughts to work for you instead of against you.

I lack the education and knowledge to be successful.

An expensive education from a prestigious university doesn't always guarantee instant success. You still have to work at it. For years, I believed that a lack of education or having extensive knowledge was an obstacle for me, until I remembered that Albert Einstein never finished high school, yet he changed the world with his vision, theories, and ideas.

It is not a lack of education that causes great failures. It is a lack of imagination.

I was brought up to be ordinary.

It is perfectly acceptable to be ordinary. In a sense, we all are just trying to do our best with what we have. When you come to realize your life's purpose, you have an opportunity to become more than just ordinary. You can do great things, but still do them in an ordinary fashion.

How you were raised only influences your outcomes to a point. You make the decision as to whether or not you want to do things the way you were trained to do them.

People who have achieved great things are still ordinary people. They are just ordinary people who accomplished great things because they committed to mastering their craft.

I have no time for my dreams.

If you have no time for your dreams, what do you have time for?

It's all been done before.

Great discoveries have been made over the last few decades that have challenged the human imagination in ways never dreamed possible a hundred years ago. It is also true that great ideas are explored every day, and sometimes we lose faith in our ideas or planning because we fear someone else already got there first.

However, it hasn't all been done before or we would be living in a world without any growing needs. The world is still in need of new ideas and visions.

Sometimes these ideas build upon what has already been created, and other times, a new door is opened, leading to future innovative ideas and dynamic pathways.

The Battle with Victim Mentality

> *"Failures, repeated failures, are finger posts on the road to achievement. One fails forward toward success."*
>
> **— C.S. Lewis.**

There are two types of failures. There are people who fail forward by taking intentional action steps in spite of the fear they are dealing with. These are the high achievers, high-level success stories, and people who get done what they wanted to get done

But another type of failing, which eludes many of us, is the victim mentality mindset. This mindset sets you up for failure as soon as it becomes activated.

Your Victim Mindset: A Pathway to Failure

We tend to believe that it is the actions taken that fail us. For example: "If only I hadn't decided to start my own business, I wouldn't have lost all that money." Or, "If I hadn't gotten married, I wouldn't be going through this messy divorce right now."

You might perceive these events as failures. But let me ask you this. At what point in this process did you feel successful? On your wedding day, didn't that feel good? Or when you had your children, the day they were born was the best day of your life? Or the first family trip to Disneyland?

Chances are you didn't think of these moments as failures. You were on top of the world. But now, 10–15 years later, it isn't working out anymore, and you and your spouse decide to part ways, and now you are certain that it was all for nothing.

The voices of negativity that were not there before emerge. You're overwhelmed by how powerful this voice is. It hammers you down until there is nothing left. You start to become a victim in your own mind, and this life that served you well has become a prison.

The one true path for failure is never trying. You believe that it is hopeless so you give up before taking action at all. There is always an excuse and a reason why you can't succeed.

I know someone who quit their job to pursue a career in music. Co-workers and friends all said she was crazy because musicians rarely make money these days. She knew the risk, but she also knew the risk of staying in a corporate job that was eating her alive. She almost went back twice that year to her job when things didn't work out or it looked like she wouldn't be able to pay her bills.

But Sara didn't back down. People around her, out of "concern", warned her of the risks of failing. After all, they would not have tried anything as radical as leaving a well-paying job. But believing that failures never take action, she persevered and went on to become a successful musician. The friends she knows are still complaining about their jobs and how they wish they could change.

But they just can't do it because...

Victim mentality is an acquired personality trait in which a person tends to recognize or consider themselves as a victim of the negative actions of others and to behave as if this were the case in the face of contrary evidence of such circumstances.

Fear can have a big impact on you. The fear of losing face or looking bad in front of people. You might return to your place of origin only to be unhappier than you were before you quit. You've got to leap and keep on flying. You haven't failed until you've given up trying and decided you are ready to settle for whatever everyone else wants.

That is failure, in knowing you have a gift, something to share with the world, and yet you're too afraid to go after it, too scared to do something about it, too paralyzed to move ahead because you keep thinking, *What if I fall down? What if they laugh at me?*

Well, they might. People will always warn you against doing something that entails some form of risk where you could lose. Why? Are they afraid you will fail?

NO. They are afraid that you'll succeed. That they are the ones who will be left behind, and you are the one who shows the rest it can be done. Some might follow you, but most won't. But soon they'll be telling people about how they once knew you.

You're so concerned about the actions you're taking? But it is the actions you are not taking that are failing you. It is your victim mentality that is causing you to fail. This mentality was formed in early childhood through a systematic process of bullying, self-defeat, criticism, or a traumatic event that has caused you to experience such deep pain, mistrust and grief that you learned to cope by feeling sorry for yourself.

I want you to know something: You have the courage and personal power to take back your life. Your mindset is a choice. You make this choice every minute of the day. Everything you have been buying into exists because you're holding on to it. If you want to be free—and I'm certain you do—here is how you do it.

How a Failure Mind Trap Governs Your Future

The course you are taking in this life right now is dependent on your mindset: Do you have a victim mentality attitude or an independent and mature attitude? Is your mind conditioned to expect failure or success? Do you perceive yourself as someone who deserves to be happy or are you confined to being miserable?

The victim is stuck in "I can't." This is the belief system that trains you to be weak, to play a weak role.

The failure mind trap is deeply ingrained in imposter syndrome and a belief that, no matter the success you have had, it is never enough. You are always climbing a ladder that leads to nowhere because there is no end to it.

Self-Sabotage

Self-sabotage is one of the ways you repeatedly fail yourself. What is self-sabotage? It is the deliberate act of ruining your chances of success before—or just after—you achieve your goal. Why would someone deliberately destroy the very thing they hope to achieve?

You might not have a victim mindset, or at least, to a large degree, you operate from a place of personal power. But do you ever feel sorry for yourself, catch yourself saying, "I just can't do this," or doubting your skills and abilities? Most of us—to some degree—fall into this trap. We revert back to moments of reflection when we were mistreated, abused, or made to look stupid.

The mind of a victim is trapped. You see yourself as someone who has been deeply wronged, and the harm done to you was undeserved and unjustified. You want sympathy and for someone to recognize what has been done.

If not treated, this builds on a mind set for self-sabotage. You feel so much mistrust, that you have been betrayed or deceived, and that you are undeserving of anything life has to offer. So much in fact that when something good does come along, you can't believe that it is actually happening to you.

You start to question your self-worth. Then you begin to doubt your self-worth. If this lingers, the next stage takes you into acting out, when you will deliberately do something to damage your success. This justifies your sense of failure and proves that you are the loser you always knew you were.

Self-sabotage is a form of intentional failure. Similar to procrastination, when your victim mindset has convinced you that you're not worthy of admiration, love, or success, it seeks to remove it, taking you back to the starting point again. At this stage you would say, "There, you see? I told you (she'd leave me/they would fire me/I couldn't pass the test)."

With failing now justified, you can stay stuck in your victim mindset, avoiding the work required to make change happen. The fact is giving up is easy. It's making the transition out of this victim mentality that is the real challenge.

Breaking Your Mental Demons

When you decide that you won't do something, you are deciding to fail before trying. This is a subconscious choice. It is your internal victim saying, "We can't do that."

Here is what happens when you listen to that negative internal dialogue of the tragic victim:

- You choose to eat fast food for the second day in a row over going to the gym.

- You choose to spend your money on expensive jewelry instead of saving for that business you want to start up or that dream trip on your bucket list.

- You choose to play with your smartphone for 30 minutes on the couch instead of going for that three-mile run.

- You choose to give in to your victim mindset instead of taking intentional action and doing that one thing that could change your life forever. Do you even know what it is?

What this boils down to is a deeper level of procrastination. Your habit to procrastinate is the single biggest obstacle standing between you and success. Why? It's easier to give in and decide "I'll do it tomorrow."

But tomorrow comes and you find another excuse. Your excuses become the normal flow to your day. When you don't want to get uncomfortable, and there are very few who do, you just reach down into your "excuses jar" and pull out the next one.

What does your victim mindset say this time?

- "I'm too tired."

- "I'll do it later when I'm feeling more energetic."

- "I tried that last time and it didn't work."

- "My knee injury isn't quite healed ... from last month."

- "I haven't eaten lunch yet."

- "I'm not good enough. My own father told me so."

- "Everyone my age is more successful than I am. What's the point?"

- "I failed so much growing up. It must be a sign."

- "There is nothing I am really good at."

Excuses ... procrastination ... a hard-core victim mentality carved into the corner of your mind. These three vices work together with one singular purpose: To rob you of a life you could have and feed you large portions of a life you're convinced you're stuck with.

Let me tell you this: *The only life you're stuck with is the one you choose to live.*

A victim mentality sets you apart from the real you. I've seen many people fail and flounder through life because they refused to get up off the floor that they had been lying on since childhood. Old voices of the past, memories that we hold on to, and past failures that have left us scarred, battle-worn, and broken.

If you continue to buy into this shit, you will spend all of your days failing. Failing at what?

Your way of life becomes a symbol of everything you stand for. It has nothing to do with the momentary achievements or brief wins. It is what you are thinking, feeling and doing right now. Your past, the place in time where your victim mindset was born and has power over you, isn't going to let go because you wish it. It's laughing at you right now because it is convinced you're too weak to fight back.

Your victim mindset has nothing to fear as long as you're afraid. It has no fear of tomorrow because it is expecting tomorrow to be like every other day with you plodding through, doing and thinking the same way, changing nothing ... and striving for nothing.

Okay, now that I've spent the last couple pages kicking your teeth in and painting the grim picture of what your future looks like trapped in this hell, are you ready to break free and get serious?

By the way, everyone has a victim mental mindset to some degree. We are all holding on to something that has us in its vices and refuses to let go. If you are not observant and don't wake up to the realization that it's there, you could end up wasting years of your life trapped.

- Trapped in relationships that are abusive or unhealthy.

- Trapped in a job that is beneath your true potential.

- Trapped in a town that you can't leave because the thought of starting a new life somewhere terrifies you.

- Trapped in a comfort zone that wants you to stay the person you are because it hates discomfort.

- Trapped in a state of suffering because you know you are meant for more than a life of boring routines and Netflix every weekend.

- Trapped in a mind that craves expansion but you are feeding it all the wrong brain food (affirmations, positive talk, etc.).

Your victim mentality, no matter how severe, can be broken. But the first step in breaking this is admitting that it's there—it has always been there feeding you lies, pretending to protect you when in fact it is shielding you from the truth.

When you see yourself living out this fixed mindset, it will kick you into overdrive. You will start doing the things that cause you fear, but you will be comfortable with that.

Fear is good. Fear means you're alive. I know lots of people say they fear nothing. I thought they were some kind of super humans, but as it turns out, they do nothing and that is why they have no fear.

Do not wait for the fear to fade before stepping out of your zone. The minute that fear makes an appearance that is your victim mentality protesting. You will go through a lot of that. It begins with excuses. Then heavy resistance if you get past the excuses.

When you turn off the old habits and break up that old record that has been playing in your mind, it is you stepping onto a new path ... and ahead of you is rough terrain, unknown obstacles, and an unpredictable way of living.

This is where failure thrives because you can only fail when you confront your fears and act anyway. You can only fail when you try something different, tackle that new challenge, or act in a way that goes against your fixed mindset.

The victim mindset lives in the world of illusion. This is how it has survived for so long. Your purpose is to expose that illusion and break it open for the world to see.

Let me share with you a story I heard once.

A man had spent the last ten years in a jail cell. Every day he sat on the floor of his cell dreaming of freedom and what it would be like to escape from his room. He never spoke to anyone and he became so accustomed to his jail cell that eventually he stopped dreaming of escape and accepted his fate.

One day, one of the new guards in the prison stood outside his cell and said, "I don't understand why you don't just leave. You could have left this room at any time."

The prisoner said, "Don't be so foolish. I have been locked in here for almost a decade. I can't leave if the door is locked all day."

The guard reached out without a key and pushed gently on the door to the prisoner's cell. It slid open without much effort.

The prisoner, realizing he was now free, was suddenly filled with a new sense of hope and purpose; life came back into his very being. He ran out of the cell never to return.

As the prisoner fled the prison, the guard said to himself, "Strange, he was free this whole time and didn't even know it."

Most of us are like that prisoner in the cage, trapped by our own beliefs into thinking there is no way out.

If this is you, you are free. You only need to give yourself permission to escape. The only option remaining is to fail throughout your life without going anywhere, doing nothing and being nothing.

Let's not go down that path. You can turn around, start over, or start on a new journey.

This won't happen immediately, but awareness is the first step. It is the master key. You open the doors to your prison as soon as you become aware the doors were never locked to begin with.

I am not going to give you any fluffy advice here and tell you to go hug a teddy bear to get in touch with your feelings. Let's get to the root of our issues so we can start to heal and move on. But hey, if you have a teddy bear, give it a squeeze.

> *"You can be discouraged by failure, or you can learn from it. So go ahead and make mistakes, make all you can. Because, remember, that's where you'll find success—*
> *on the far side of failure."*
>
> **— Thomas J. Watson**

The Price of Living with Your Victim Mindset

Failing is a good thing when it proves to be a teacher. When you buy into your failure as a hindrance and it becomes your default, you are paying for this.

When you believe that you are victimized, you validate this truth with false beliefs. You look for the evidence that justifies your attitude. This makes it hard to change.

Ask yourself this question: "What is the cost for holding on to this victim mentality?"

Here is what it's costing you:

- A life of solitude and isolation. You fail to develop relationships when you are a victim.

- Giving up the dream you could have. Victims are not living out their dreams but trapped in a pattern of entitlement.

- A life of scarcity. You are never happy with what you have and are always wanting more to fill up your inner emptiness.

The price for living with your victim attitude is your life itself. As you carry self-pity with you, blaming and looking for people to save you, you are losing opportunity, freedom and a life that could be everything and more.

Don't take the victim mentality path. It won't end well.

Action Tip: Based on the examples I provided here, I want you to think about the negative cost of everything you stand to lose. Use this as leverage and turn it around so that you are developing an empowered attitude.

Failure Redirect: Dealing with Failure That Isn't Yours

> *"You won't believe what you can accomplish by attempting the impossible with the courage to repeatedly fail better."*
>
> — **Tim Ferriss**

Many of your failings come about by your own actions. You made a snap decision resulting in a failed outcome. You invested 50k in a new business venture that fell through, taking your cash with it. Your marriage fell apart after one year because you had an affair. Failure by your own actions hurts. But, there is another version of failure that takes place. It's the failure brought about by the carelessness or intent of others.

Have you ever had to deal with a difficult situation because someone else messed up?

How do you deal with failure when it's brought on by another person's actions? How do you handle it when someone else fails you, and you end up with the losses? This could be the actions of a family member, friend, or people in your organization.

When it's your own fault, you can say, "I did this, so it's my fault." But when you suffer a setback—financial, emotional or physical harm—because of another person's mistake, negligence or purposeful intent, it becomes harder to accept. Your first reaction is to blame and complain to others that he did this, or she said that, and then you move into the victim role.

But a victim is a helpless soul that needs protection. A victim becomes paralyzed with grief. A victim wants resolution. While there are various kinds of victim roles, if someone does something to you that creates a loss or sets you back, how you handle it— your perspective towards the situation—determines if you come out of it on top.

Here is a case to explain this:

Don and Joe set up a business together. They ran the business for nearly 10 years and, over the course of this time, had accumulated a large customer base and employed 15 people full-time. Then, the business started going through hard times. Clients dropped off and went with the competition, and the business owners were forced to lay off several of their workers. And then Joe, Don's partner, disappeared one day.

He took most of the money out of the company's account and had also taken off with one of the women that worked in the company from the beginning. Together, they had devised a plan to escape, taking most of Don's assets with them. They were never seen again.

But now, Don had a failing company, no cash to back it up, and the remaining employees who were still working full-time needed to be paid.

He was angry at first. Who wouldn't be? The partner he had trusted for a decade betrayed him, stole his business, and ran off with his most valuable worker, leaving him broken, broke, and alone.

Don lapsed into a depression, blaming himself for not seeing this coming. But as many people know, the knockout punch always hits you in the area you are not protecting. Don was so engrossed in keeping things afloat, and dealing with personal issues on top of this, that he had stopped communicating with his partner.

In the midst of all this, when things couldn't get worse, they did. Several months later, as the company grew smaller in profit and clientele, Don was unable to pay the bills. Several more employees quit, and he was unable to hire anyone else because, after all, who wants to work for someone that can't pay the bills?

Not soon after, Don's only brother died. His brother had been like a mentor to him and with the only person he could talk to now gone, he was truly alone. The house was collapsing. Failure was imminent. He considered filing for bankruptcy. The only solution he could see was losing everything and starting over.

But Don had everything invested in this. He needed time to think, to reconnect, and to think of solutions. He was immersed in the obsessiveness of failing. He had many friends who had failed before. Some rebuilt what they had lost. Others lost it and never rebuilt. He wasn't sure what side of the fence he would end up on, but he was certain that giving up was not an option. He might fail, but he would not fail by throwing it all in.

> *"Mistakes are a fact of life.*
> *It is the response to error that counts."*
>
> **— Nikki Giovanni**

As he stepped away for a week to gain his mind back and focus his mindset on the situation, he was able to realize that he was blaming himself for this failure. Self-blame, low confidence and feeling demoralized by his failure was the main cause for the downward spiral he was stuck in. Don realized that if he didn't pull himself out of it, bounce back and learn from the experience, failure was imminent.

Don consulted in a mentor for support. He needed help and asking for it was difficult. Many people, when faced with a difficult situation, isolate and withdraw. They become shameful and they want to give up. The mind is very persuasive. It's the #1 enemy responsible for killing dreams. But only if you allow it to.

You are responsible for your own attitude. You can choose how to respond to your situation. Will you let fear push you down so far that you become paralyzed and helpless? Will you blame bad luck and throw away any hope of recovery? Can you live with the consequences of your decision?

Don's mentor had been through failings in the past. He simply said one day, "Blame, shame and not owning your responsibility will kill your mindset and destroy your attitude. You must change these things and everything else will fall into place. And even if you still fail after that, you're left with a strong mindset and positive attitude. That's all you need to rebuild."

Don went into a level of deep thinking he'd never tried before. He then asked himself two questions:

1. Who am I blaming for this?

2. What action can I take right now to change this situation and make an improvement today?

The first question forced him to look inside himself and realize that the root cause for the spiral he was in had nothing to do with his partner running off with his best employee and stealing the money. This wasn't a situation he had any control over. Even if they are caught and brought to justice, they are still gone either way.

He came to realize he had direct control over his own mind and how he decided to play the next move. He had been walking around attracting sympathy from people who knew the truth. One person even said, "It's okay if you give in. Everyone would understand. Most people wouldn't want to go through this."

Don found himself believing in those words. But when he began to analyze the situation, he knew something that most others didn't: he wasn't like most people. He never was. That is why he had been given this task. Because he could handle it.

He was strong. He had been through tough times before, just never a failure on this level when it all seemed to be coming unglued. He had two choices: close the business and take the losses, or see it through to the end and recover from an impossible situation.

The next morning, when the staff arrived, and morale was at an all-time low, he called a meeting. He laid out a plan to bring the business back. It wouldn't be easy, but they would rebound. Anyone who wanted out now would receive a month's severance and no hard feelings. Two people left but the rest stayed. They looked hopeful and Don could trust them.

The second question is what fueled everyone to work hard for what they believed: "What is the one thing I can do today that will shift the odds in my favor?" In Gary Keller's book—The One Thing—he calls this the "Focusing Question".

It is a powerful question. It gets your mind off the failures of the past. It moves you away from feeling sorry for yourself and mentally preparing to give up. Instead, you choose not to take the easy way and mentally get up after the knockdown.

Ask yourself: "What is the ONE action I can take today that will change everything from here on in?"

This requires us to let go of the past. It is a call to your present moment and coming into the realization that the only decision that matters is the highest decision you can make now. Ultimately, what you choose to focus on becomes your reality.

In Don's case, he was fixated on blame and feeling like a victim. This made him weak when he should have been strong. But as soon as he took a proactive choice and owned the situation, it turned around. His partner was not coming back. The business had lost several employees. But they still had customers that needed to be taken care of, and in spite of the internal crisis, business was on an upswing.

In fact, after Don was able to take off the "victim blinders" and change his attitude to a proactive stance, good things began to happen. He renegotiated with the bank on the business loan and was given a line of credit to consolidate expenses. By turning his attention towards the real people that ran the business—his customer base—his clientele increased by 13% in the first 3 months. And then increased by 27% only 6 months after that. For the staff that stayed, although paying salaries had been a challenge, in the midst of all this, he gave everyone a 10% raise.

On reflection, Don learned two important lessons from this experience: 1. Circumstances are always beyond your control. 2. You can only change your reaction to those circumstances.

Yes, he wasn't responsible for what his partner had done, but he could decide how he would react. Will you sit down and drown in pity, looking for sympathy while your world falls apart? Or will you get up and do what needs to be done?

Failure happens to everyone, and in many cases, not by your own doing. Look at the situation and ask yourself, "What can I do about this? What action is available right now? Who can I talk to about developing a positive solution to this crisis?"

You have control over your choices in the present moment, and not in the past or the future. Failure can impact you negatively if you allow it to. It can kill self-esteem and drain your confidence. This leads to failure expectation, the path of self-sabotage, and makes many people create barriers to success.

You are not always responsible for the circumstances that are thrown at you. You are responsible for how you react to them. You own the right to fight or walk away. You owe it to yourself to dig in and not give in to the crippled mind that takes the side of fear.

Where many people see failure as a curse or hindrance, you can approach it from a different angle. It is your greatest learning curve and will teach you more about how to stay focused and strong than you could ever know.

Handling Indirect Failure

Let me ask you this: what would you do? In a situation where you lose it all, and just when it couldn't get worse, you lose a little more. How much would you have to lose before you break? Life is full of challenges, but we never know to what level we will be challenged until it happens.

With challenges comes opportunity. By working through your situation and taking ownership of what you can influence, and being honest with yourself about your situation, it empowers you to seek a way out of your mess. Instead of sitting in the middle of your crisis feeling like it's all coming to an end, you empower your mind to take immediate action on a small task. This can be anything, but it should be an actionable step that gets you out of your rut.

In Don's situation, he recognized what he could control and made attempts to focus on that, instead of the people and circumstances he couldn't change.

(1). Control Your Initial Reaction: Anger

Suffering through a heavy setback impacts people in different ways. At first, there is shock, then disbelief, and often denial about what is happening. I have seen people stuck in denial for a long time. When this happens, it becomes impossible to break free of this mindset unless you have help.

Your reaction could be to get angry, and anger leads to resentment. Resentment leads to negative thoughts, blame and a disempowering feeling of helplessness.

It is easy to express anger at your situation. You want to get even. You want to hold someone responsible. You justify your anger because someone took advantage of you.

But anger is a reaction that moves you away from working on a solution to the problem. Of course, you initially feel angry. But when you hold onto it and let it burn, simmering beneath the surface, it can turn into resentment. Sometimes rage. Anger is your emotions losing control. It leads you away from taking control and owning responsibility.

You need to turn that anger into determination. You decide to make a mental shift in your mind. If your emotions are a choice, you can decide to hold onto this anger and let it control you. Or you can let it go, give it up, and make a decision to not let it permeate your mind.

(2). Forge an Unbreakable Positive Attitude

Throughout this book, and the Fail Big series, I make repetitive references to the importance of a positive attitude. This is because I truly believe it is the ultimate weapon when faced with adversity.

Napoleon Hill, author of *Keys to Success*, said this about positive attitude development:

> *"Realize, and prove to your own satisfaction by making it so, that every adversity, sorrow, or defeat, whether or not you caused it to happen, contains the seed of an equivalent benefit which you can nurture into a blessing that soars above the disaster that brought it."*

Your attitude will drive decisions and lead your actions. When you find yourself on the losing end of a bad situation, how will you make it right? What will be your attitude when failure is forcing your mindset to convert to giving up?

Your attitude is the #1 thing you have direct control over at any given time, no matter the situation. It is the only force that is under your control at all times, no matter what is happening around you. Attitude makes or breaks you. It determines who survives and who dies, who wins or who loses.

You can't undo what has been done, but the winning moment is when you can have the courage to move past the pain of losing. You may not have created this situation, but you will deal with it. And when you're finished, you will have made the best of a failed situation.

> *"Failures, repeated failures, are finger posts on the road to achievement. One fails forward toward success."*
>
> ## — C.S. Lewis

Let's take a look at **Viktor Frankl**. He was a survivor of Hitler's death camps, having been a prisoner from 1942-1945. Viktor was separated from his wife and family when they were sent to the camps. He never saw them again, but always held onto the hope they were alive.

In the camps, Viktor was exposed to conditions that most people would never see or fathom happening. Death was a real possibility every waking moment. The cold was killing hundreds a day. Starvation, depression and disease were as common as the rats.

And during these times of darkness, Viktor was one of the few who survived. How?

Viktor created this belief:

> *"Everything can be taken from a man but one thing: the last of the human freedoms—to choose one's attitude in any given set of circumstances, to choose one's own way."*

Viktor knew he couldn't change his external situation. He couldn't end the war or influence his capturers to set him free. But he could control the way he perceived the situation. And that is what he did.

If a man who lost everything with almost no chance of survival is able to maintain this attitude, what is stopping you?

Here are **5 steps** to building a positive mental attitude:

1. Release the blame you're holding onto for all past failures. Focus intensely on the action you can take today.

2. Identify the #1 goal you are working toward. Make it your mission to direct your thoughts and efforts towards reaching this goal.

3. Hire your mentor. Contact this person directly and meet with him or her once a week.

4. Provide your services to another who is going through hard times. You can provide your time or direct that person to reading a good book, watching an interview with an inspirational speaker, or listening to their story. You have the power to change lives.

5. Always be learning. A mind that sits still slides back and gets sidetracked into creating worrisome thoughts. Write down positive quotes in a journal and read these frequently.

(3). Identifying Controllable Action

Many happenings, situations, or in the case of a global crisis, we have no control over. But what you can do is identify the actions taken by you based on your decision.

Make a list of ten things that you have no control over. Here is my list:

1. Earthquakes

2. Other people's choices

3. Stock market crashing

4. Winter freeze in Canada

5. Flu pandemic

6. Company going bankrupt because the CEO made a bad business decision

7. Tax increase

8. Your wife/husband deciding to leave you

9. Pets dying

10. Children growing up.

There are so many events, conditions and uncontrollable circumstances that, after making your list, you come to realize daily living is made up of 90% stuff you have no control over. If you did, you'd be able to:

1. Prevent earthquakes

2. Stop people from making choices you don't like

3. Shift the stock market in your favor

4. Turn up the heat in Canada

5. Come up with a cure for the epidemic

6. Stop the CEO from making poor decisions, or fire him/her before they can make a bad one.

7. Tell the government to stop the tax increase

8. Stop your spouse from leaving

9. Increase your pet's longevity by another ten years

10. Tell your kids to stick around forever.

Yes, silly, right? Yet, when change occurs, don't we complain about it as if change shouldn't be happening? Living is living through the constant shifting of events. Good things happen, bad things happen, and how you perceive it comes down to your attitude towards the change.

Make a list of what you can control. The list is much shorter I can tell you.

Here is what I can control at the end of the day:

1. My mindset/attitude

2. My own decisions (what can I do?).

Make your list of what you can control, and remind yourself what that is. Then, when an event does happen to you (and it happens every day), you aren't stuck in pity or complaining about circumstances beyond your control. You will be much happier, more productive, and better focused on creating a purpose-driven lifestyle.

(4). Fix Your Efforts on Healing.

It takes time to heal. When you find yourself in a difficult situation that you didn't create, know that you are still a part of this. Your goal is to be stepping up and not down. You can do this by exercising your free will. Free will is your right to say, "Yes, I've got this."

When people enter into recovery, it isn't because someone is forcing them to make this move. Yes, there could be interventions and concerned friends reaching out, but recovering from a bad fall begins with you deciding to stand up and continue the fight. The people who break through failing—who can stand everything life throws at them—will persevere and come out on top in the end.

Failing Fast in Motion:

1. Turn your failure into a positive experience.

How can you turn this situation into a positive experience?

2. Determine what you could have done differently.

What different choices could have been made?

3. Work with someone you trust to plan out a comeback.

Who do you know that can help you bring this back?

4. Decide if you will allow this setback to win.

Will you let failure win, or can you gather the strength to push over this failure?

Reduce Your Failure Rate

> *"I've missed more than 9,000 shots in my career. I've lost almost 300 games. 26 times I've been trusted to take the game's winning shot and missed. I've failed over and over and over again in my life and that's why I succeed."*

> — **Michael Jordan**

Failing isn't something you can avoid. There are events and circumstances beyond your control. Trying to stop yourself from failing would mean to take no risks, do nothing, have no aspirations, and spend all your time sitting in the "safety zone" watching life happen.

There is no such thing as a *fail free* life.

But, you can eliminate the risk factor. How many times have you been caught off guard because you forgot to plan ahead? Think about many of the mishaps or failures you've had in the past and what you could have done to reduce the loss or damage. How can you reduce the chance of making the same mistake twice? What obstacles do you see ahead that you could plan for?

Many of your obstacles become barriers to success because you fail to see the problem until it's too late. While you can't predict everything that is going to happen, you can plan better for future challenges by upgrading skills, saving more money, and thinking about possible scenarios down the road. As a good friend of mine once said: "The best time to fill up your car is when the tank is ¾ full." Don't wait until the last minute to prepare for a failing moment as it's knocking on your front door. You can accelerate your growth and development by preparing for difficulty.

It is hard to learn from life's mistakes when you repeat the same mistakes again and again. You say, "next time will be different," and yet, you repeat the exact habit that leads to the same outcome.

How many times have you said, "If only I had been ready, I could have avoided losing...

- My money
- My time
- My relationship
- My reputation
- My health
- My career

You can't avoid falling down, but you can reduce your losses by not falling as hard. There are no lessons in failing if you continue to make the same mistakes and do nothing to change it. We all fail in different ways.

Failure is a good thing because it teaches you the lessons needed to grow. This is why you must be open to changing your habits, behavior and way of thinking.

If you continue to repeatedly perform the same action, you will produce the same result.

A First Lesson in Failure

In a workshop I attended recently, the discussion of "how to overcome the fear of failure" was brought up as one of the primary themes. The class was given a short assignment. Each of the attendees would have 2 minutes to address everyone and talk about their fear of failure, and how it negatively impacted their lives.

One of the participants, when it got to be his turn, simply said, *"Look, we all know failing is inevitable, it's what we do to prevent failure that matters. It isn't failing that scares me, but I just want to know, how can I fail less?"* In other words, he was asking: *"How can I reduce the amount I fail in the future by being more observant and taking immediate action today?"*

Knowing failure is a common fear and that it is something we all struggle with, I started drafting out a list of strategies that people could implement to prevent failing—and falling—as hard.

The idea to 'Reduce Your Failure Rate' is a concept I learned from a friend of mine who has a health clinic. As a naturopath, she teaches her patients the best way to stay healthy through proper dieting, nutrition and exercise. She teaches people how to live happy, healthier lives by preventing disease *before* it happens. Her motto is, *"The best time to fight cancer is ten years before you're diagnosed."*

> *"Yesterday is gone. Tomorrow has not yet come. We only have today. Let us begin."*
>
> ## — Mother Teresa

The best time to deal with failing is to do something today in order to reduce your failure rate for the next 10-20 years. Similar to someone who would start by changing their diet and doing everything possible to reduce their risk of cancer, you can take charge today by predicting the areas of your life that are at risk.

If you want to 'predict' your future, you have to start planning for it today. Can you visualize the roadblocks ahead? Are your current habits preparing you for success, or setting you up for failure?

If you want to reduce your rate of failure, you have to start now by focusing on the areas of your life that are at risk.

For example:

- Is your health at risk from eating too much junk?
- Is your business at risk because you're not keeping financial records up to date?
- Is your relationship at risk because you're not communicating enough?
- Is your mental health deteriorating because you're watching too much TV or playing games?

Remember this: Failure is not a one-time event that suddenly happens to you. You fail throughout life by not acting accordingly. It's the decisions you make today—in this moment—that decide if you will succeed or fail in the future.

Using the above examples again:

- Your health will fail because you decide to eat junk today.
- Your business will fail because you're not managing your books today
- Your relationship will fail because you're ignoring your partner…again.
- Your mental health is weakening because you will watch three hours of Netflix instead of reading or meditating.

Now, here are 7 strategies to help reduce your failure rate.

(1). Spend Quality Time with 5 Successful People

You are the average of the people you spend the most time with. This is why it is critical to spend quality time with the people supporting you and helping each other. This could be your team at work, family at home, or your close circle of friends. The people you spend quality time with empower you for success.

Your support team are the people who are there for you when you need them, and they need you. They don't let you give up or make excuses for not getting things done. They'll be there for you when life gets in the way and you need that extra push, a close talk, and the knowing they are there for you through the thick of it all.

Be observant of the people who are trying to hold you back. They may ask you, "Why are you doing this?" or "What's gotten into you?" We have to realize people are still struggling with their own demons and personal trials.

The people you spend time with is an investment, in your life and in theirs, too. Look around you at the five people you are with most of the time. Do you trust them? Can you talk openly and honestly with these people? Are they willing to go the distance with you in difficult times?

We all want that "dream team" of people who are there to support us Find a mentor or accountability partner whom you can lean on for support. A mentor can be there to guide you through rough times when you're struggling. Hire a life coach and have weekly sessions so you stay on track with your goals.

(2). Identify Your Achilles' Heel

In Greek mythology, Achilles was a Greek hero of the Trojan War. According to legend, Achilles—who was a powerful warrior and believed to be undefeatable—was killed after being shot in the heel by an arrow. Not even Achilles could have predicted this was how he was going to die. If Achilles had known beforehand this was his only vulnerable spot, he could have planned ahead to protect himself during the Trojan War. He was shot in the heel by an arrow and died.

We have areas in our lives in which we are not strong, and while it may not kill us—as it did Achilles—we could end up setting ourselves up for failure by not recognizing what that is.

In many situations when defeat is prominent, it is our inability to see what's coming that defeats us. It is this weak link that throws us off-balance. Not setting ourselves up for success before our biggest challenge is at hand can result in losing the battle before it begins.

You have a weak link that is setting you up for failure. You don't know what it is yet, but it's there. It sets us up for the fall and hits us when we least expect it. This could be a lack of awareness, a bad habit, an addiction not yet dealt with, or an old self-defeating belief.

Here are the top 9 "Achilles' Heels" people struggle to overcome. See if yours is on the list:

1. Overconfidence
2. Lack of Knowledge
3. Procrastination
4. Poor Health
5. Underestimating Your Opponent
6. Scattered Focus
7. Lack of Attention

8. Negative Mindset
9. Limited Thought Patterns

You won't always see defeat coming, but you can prevent it the best you can by taking these measures to reduce your chances of failing:

Beat Your Achilles' Heel

Step 1: Look back and make a note of the last three setbacks you have had. Do these setbacks have something in common?

Step 2: what is the one area of your life in which you fail on a consistent basis? Is it your health? Relationships? The area of your life bringing you the most grief is telling you that there is a problem.

Step 3: Make a list of the solutions you could start to work with. In the case of my procrastination habit, I made a list of tasks I had been putting off. I had things on my list dating back years. I was paying for it with guilt. Now, what can you do? What is the one small action you can take today?

Step 4: Make this daily action a habit. Create a trigger, so you recognize when it is acting up.

Step 5: Be sure to recognize the positive changes in your life by taking action. How do you feel emotionally? Are you more confident, at peace, or your mind is quitter than before?

Step 6: Continue to focus on developing a system of continuous self-improvement. Don't let yourself fail.

Don't be caught off-guard. Be ready for when that day comes, and you know life is going to get the best of you. Fight back and get up when you get knocked down.

You will always have a weak link in your routine, habits, or way of thinking. Make a list of what these weak links are and keep working on eliminating them.

(4). Plan for the Future...Today

If you fail to plan in the present, you plan to fail in the future. Although I admit most of my thinking is centered in the present moment, I do have to plan for the future by taking care of business in the now.

For example, now is the time to eat healthy, not in twenty years when you're diagnosed with an illness. Now is the time to train and exercise, and not later when you're fifty pounds overweight. Now is the time to plan for your financial future, and not five years before retirement. Now is the time to develop your relationships with your children, and not in ten years when they don't want to spend time with you anymore.

You should spend one hour a week reviewing your goals for the next year, month, week, and day. Time-block in one hour every Sunday afternoon or evening and drill down into your plans. Are your projects up to date? Have you submitted the papers you filled out? Is there anything that came up this week you need to put into your planning funnel?

This hour could the most important hour of your week. If you want to do this right, I recommend you build this system into your routine. Make it a solid habit. Buy a yearly planner and a wall calendar. I am using Michael Hyatt's *Full Focus Planner* so I can map out my weeks ahead of time. All the organizing is done for you so you just have to fill in the tasks.

Ask yourself:

- Who are you spending time with this week?
- What is your top 3 goals for the week/month?
- How much sleep do you want to get each night?
- What exercise are you going to do, when, and how long will each training session be?
- What would you like to learn today so you can grow your business by 10-20% over the next year?

"By failing to prepare, you are preparing to fail."

(5). Ask for Help

One of the hardest things to do is ask for help. We are afraid of being rejected. If you don't ask, you don't get. And we need to elicit the help of others to get to where we want to be.

Think about all the things you are not asking for in your life. Chances are, you could fill up a page. Right now, take out a piece of paper and make a list of all the things you want to ask for, but have always been afraid to.

Here are some prompts to get you moving:

- "What am I afraid to ask my spouse for?"
- "What am I afraid to ask my best friend for?"
- "What am I afraid to ask total strangers for?"
- "What am I afraid to ask my mentor for?"
- "What am I afraid to ask my manager for?"
- "What am I afraid to ask myself for?"

Everyone has something they are afraid to ask for. Once you clearly identify the things you are afraid to ask for, you can move forward with the next phase:

"Why?"

Next to the list of things you are afraid to ask for, write down the reason why you are afraid to ask. This is the fuel that will move you into doing something about it. Knowing what you are afraid to ask for is the first step. It brings clarity to what you are hiding from. But the why should make you see how silly the fear is, and prompt you to push through it.

Here is my **simple 6-step process** for asking for what you want:

1. Write down—in a notebook or using the Evernote app—the one thing you really want.

2. Make a short list of three people who could provide this.
3. Write down the benefit you are providing by asking them for what you desire to have.
4. Ask confidently, as if it is already yours.
5. Be respectful of their decision if it doesn't turn out the way you wanted.
6. Finally, let go of your expectations.

You can make a massive difference in your life by asking the right people for the right things at the right time. Commit to asking for at least one thing you desire a day. This can be something you want for yourself, or better yet, to help someone else obtain something they want.

Visualize the one thing you asked for being given to you. That job you want, the loan, a promise, or a three-week vacation. Yes, anything is yours the moment you get the courage to ask for it. If you get refused? That is good. You now develop tougher skin for asking again.

(6) Consistently Improve by 1%

Where would you be one year from now if you focused on making small adjustments to your habits, thoughts, systems, or behavior by just 1%? Do you think this is a low % to shoot for? Why not be more ambitious and go for 20%?

Here is a strategy you can implement that contributes continuously towards your growth rate without creating an obstacle or feeling of overwhelm. If you've ever crammed for a test by trying to do all the studying the night before, you know what this feels like.

If you joined a marathon for the first time, would you start training several days before the event? This wouldn't be enough time. But, if you start training 4-6 months before and begin by running 1km a day, within two months, you will be conditioned to go the distance.

You can achieve most goals by applying the 1% rule. I often hear people say things like:

"I have no time to read."

"If only I had an extra hour."

You only have to read for ten minutes a night. Read 3 pages if you can. If you don't have 30-60 minutes, invest the time you can when you can.

I can't get to the gym every night. So, it's tough to exercise at all. You don't need a gym. You can work out at home. In twenty minutes, you could do push-ups, pull-ups, or stretching. If you need to go to the gym, you go when you can, but when it's impossible, make it possible at home.

By doing the minimum, you are still working on the habit of showing up and not buying into your excuses of, "I can't because…"

You always can, even if it is just 1%.

(7) ABP—Always Be Prepared

I believe the single biggest reason people fail is from lack of planning. Failure always trails behind the person who is least prepared. If this is you, you're an easy target.

In order to reduce your rate of failing tomorrow, next week, and in the next decade, you want to prepare yourself by taking action today. Lack of action means lack of results.

I know someone who recently lost a relative. This relative was reasonably wealthy and when he passed away, he did so without a will. They had nothing to go by. No planning or discussion had taken place to prepare for this. In the end, the estate ended up in the hands of the state. Gone.

It pays to plan. Always. Always be prepared. I strongly encourage you to spend time every day, even if it is just for ten minutes, to look at the areas of your life where you are not ready for the unexpected. When the worst-case scenario comes raining down, will you be ready?

Make sure that you:

- Get health checks regularly. Don't wait until it is too late to do something about your health.
- Revise your financial plan. Do you want to work until you're 85 paying off debt? Start your financial plan today.
- Discuss the reality of dying with your family.
- Continue to learn new skills. You never know if you will show up at work one day and no longer have a job.
- Have a small, spare gas tank in the trunk with a spare tire. Take it from my experience, you don't want to be stranded in the middle of nowhere wishing you had filled up the gas tank yesterday.

Remember this: **If you don't have a plan for your future, rest assured, somebody else does**.

Failing Fast in Motion

- Figure out what you want.
- Identify obstacles and work on one at a time.
- Take a small step toward making your vision a reality.
- Ask the right people for help.
- Take time out to think about what you learned recently, and continue to improve on these lessons.
- Build this learning into your weekly planning
- ABP—Always Be Prepared.

The Fear of Failure and Becoming *Rejection Free*

"You may have a fresh start any moment you choose, for this thing that we call 'failure' is not the falling down, but the staying down."

— Mary Pickford

Where would failure be without fear? Or how about rejection? Have you ever been rejected to the point when you were convinced failure was your destiny? When it comes to learning how to handle failure, both fear and rejection are two inseparable dynamics.

Fear is a dominating force that, if not challenged, will prevent you from taking your first leap forward. Rejection, if you let it, will become a permanent obstacle to success. You can try to go around it, or wait for the fear of rejection to subside, but fear turns to anxiety, and this reinforces your fear of failure.

When you believe in your fears more than the possibility to succeed, fear wins, and you fail by default. Your fears either block you from taking action or scare you so badly the only choice you have is to take a course of action.

This is what J.K. Rowling, bestselling author of the **Harry Potter** series, says about fear:

"It is impossible to live without failing at something unless you live so cautiously that you might as well not have lived at all, in which case you have failed by default."

Are you living your life so cautiously that failure becomes the only path possible? To fail, if you ask someone who is living their dream, means living a life that is not your own but governed by someone else's agenda. You are trapped when you believe your choices are no longer your own.

The Fear of Failure

The fear of failure is called atychiphobia. You might not perceive yourself as having a phobia when it comes to failure, but, in my experience, if you are failing in your life because of fear, phobia or not, it is an obstacle that must be eliminated if you are to crush it moving forward.

The Fears That Force Us into Failure

Atychiphobia is an abnormal, unwarranted, and persistent fear of failure. **Atychiphobia** eventually leads to a constricted lifestyle with damaging long-term impact as it keeps people removed from taking part in any activities that could lead to failing. It is an intense form of mental paralysis.

It is a persistent fear of failure that can be triggered depending on the situation you are facing.

The fear of failure has a voice, and it speaks to you like this:

- "You're just a stupid person, and you'll never succeed."
- "Everyone is smarter than you, so you have to lie to measure up."
- "You don't have what it takes to get ahead."
- "You're incompetent. If you haven't gotten it by now, you never will."
- "Everyone around you is on top. They are go-getters. You are lazy and nothing works out for you. Everything I've tried I gave up on after the first try."
- "What's the point?"
- "That's a risk you don't need. Play it safe and see how it works out."
- You're trying to be something you really aren't." (Imposter Syndrome)

So, you reinforce the fear of failure through escape. You stay below the radar, out of sight, protecting your vulnerability from cracking. You avoid situations that challenge your fears or there is the chance of your failure being exposed. It is your avoidance that widens the gap between the person you could be and who you are.

If an opportunity presents itself, you let it pass by. If you are invited to partake in an event, you turn it down. Avoidance is what makes you fail harder. You procrastinate, evade responsibility and make excuses as to why you can't. Evasion becomes self-sabotage. It all falls apart until your life is so constricted you end up living in a prison of your own making.

Failure is present in every area of our lives, and if allowed to run rampant without restraint, it makes its own rules. At home we are failures in front of our parents or siblings, at work your co-workers and even your boss, and within ourselves we are dealing with failure at an intense level because we bottle it up. Who wants to let the fear out of the cage?

If you're ready, let's dive into the fear of failure mindset and disengage this monster.

Darlene and Social Exclusion

Darlene has an intense fear of social activities. She regularly has to attend social functions as part of her job to meet with clients and drive sales for her company. Before every social function, she prepares herself mentally by recanting positive affirmations and meditating for 20–30 minutes before the party.

She does this because she deals with failure on a deep emotional level. It's the fear of measuring up to others. For most of her life, growing up Darlene had a learning disability in school, so she was treated differently and was separated into a special class. As it turns out, her learning disability was ADD, but when treated the same as the other kids, she could outperform most of them.

Darlene struggled to engage with people because she always had the negative internal belief that she wasn't good enough. In social situations, people loved to brag about their positions in the company, the schools they were educated at, and the money they were going to earn over the next few years.

Her biggest fear was not in having these conversations, but when someone asked Darlene about her background, she felt compelled to lie or exaggerate her accomplishments. She had a mindset trap that she didn't fit in and that she was never good enough. Everyone had more education, made more money, and had these big corporate jobs in fortune 500 companies. In fact, she didn't belong at all in these situations.

Before the events she had to prime herself to get through them. But what Darlene discovered is that her fear of failure, her fears of not being good enough, was internalized. When these people went home at the end of the day, they were just like everyone else: Some had families, others had nobody. They, too, were scared and that is why they had the need to brag about all their achievements.

Having a passion for stoicism, Darlene learned to be silent. She also stopped trying to impress people or make friends with the super-elite. She could be who she was and if they didn't like it, they could piss off. In reframing people, she was able to walk into any situation and feel confident, energetic, and comfortable. No more lies or shadows to hide behind.

The fear of failure is heavily immersed in fears of vulnerability, shame, unrelenting standards, comparisons to others, and deep-seated feelings of unworthiness.

If we talk about Atychiphobia, it is a combination of several—or all—of these elements.

Normally, someone in Darlene's situation would handle the situation very easily: Avoiding any kind of social situation where the risk of looking like a fool is a possibility. The downside to this is you fail to make new relationships. You fail to grow as isolation becomes your companion. And worst of all, you never outgrow this fear.

The longer you avoid challenging this fear, the stronger it takes hold. You hate to be isolated, but it is better than the alternative.

If you noticed, in Darlene's situation, she didn't change anything about her circumstances, except for one thing: Her **attitude**. She shifted and reframed the circumstances.

The result was an immediate shift in her attitude and perspective. Everything about her achievements, wealth, and social status remained the same. She no longer tried to impress anyone.

Atychiphobia (from the Greek phóbos, meaning `fear` or `morbid fear`, and atyches meaning `unfortunate`) is the abnormal, unwarranted, and persistent fear of failure.

Your fears, once identified, can be an encouraging motivator. By turning your fears into positive experiences instead of negative ones, you can flip your fear of failure into your own success story.

Your fear could be an obstacle preventing you from pushing ahead with your plans. You try to take a step forward and a voice in your head shouts, "Wait! That isn't a good idea. What if...?" And the fear sets in.

We fear failure because in the past, either in school or through our upbringing, making critical mistakes was frowned upon.

To fail is to be a failure. It brings shame. You are embarrassed in front of your friends, family and mentors. You have to be careful from now on. "Take caution," people would tell you. Perhaps you wanted to try something new and exciting, but someone always reminded you through their own fears that what you were planning to do could turn out badly. You might lose money, become humiliated, or risk your future.

So, your fears became indicators to avoid all risky propositions. Avoid ideas or big goals that had the probability of not working out. Avoid anything that had a less than likely chance of succeeding.

But where does that leave you? Without challenging the impossible or questioning the fears when they arrive, you are at the mercy of going with the flow or buying into the ideals of other people who are projecting their fears on to you.

Your fears, no matter what they are or where they come from, must be challenged. They are built false beliefs of expected negative outcomes that may or may not happen. As Jack Canfield said, "Everything you want is on the other side of fear."

If you take a chance on a business venture and invest a large sum of money, the reality is you could lose that money. But if the business succeeds, you could come out of it with everything you've ever wanted.

On one side, you risk losing your money. On the other side of fear, you succeed and live your dream for the rest of your life.

You must decide if the risk is worth the reward. Or better yet, the life you will have to live without your dreams after deciding to do nothing.

Now, let's look at the five fears that could be causing you to fail. I will cover these in more depth in the rest of the book too.

(1). Fears about what other people think

We are all afraid of risk but not just our own risks. When you see a friend doing something that could cause him or her loss, you might warn them about the possible consequences. You have heard it before:

"Be careful, you remember what happened to…"

"Are you sure you know what you're doing? That is a big chance to take…"

"When you fail, don't say I didn't warn you…"

"Nobody has ever done that before. Just be careful…"

When you try something different that hasn't been tested and the possibility of losing is high, people will always warn you to "slow down" or "think things through." It isn't that they are afraid you will fail but, rather, that you might succeed.

Your success is a mirrored reflection of the fears they are holding on to. When you fail and people see this, they are okay with that; "You see, I told you it was risky. I warned you. Now come back to reality."

But when you work towards a big goal and you hit your mark months or years later, you will silence the critics that warn you of impending doom. You can embrace the fear surrounding you and silence those who don't believe.

When you listen to the warnings of others, and believe that the fears they project on to you are real, you buy into the truth that this is a bad idea. "I should keep my head down and go with the crowd."

But that's not why we are here. You picked up this book and made it this far because you are NOT that person. You are embracing your fears, facing failure every day, and turning away from the voices of those people who are not ready to accept what you are doing.

But you know the risk is worth the reward. By avoiding the fear of failing, you shrink back into doing the same things and eventually someday regretting the risk you never took.

Who cares what other people think? Let your friends, family and co-workers throw out opinions and wait for you to fail. It isn't that they don't care. They are concerned you might actually make it and then leave them alone.

176 · SCOTT ALLAN

The Fear of Rejection

Rejection stems from the core belief that we are not worthy. People who struggle with rejection typically have low self-esteem and place little value on themselves. You might feel that you are rejected by your peers, family, or your spouse. Rejection can show up anywhere in your life.

It is a basic need for everyone to feel loved, accepted, valued, wanted, and appreciated. If we don't get these things, we go through a rejection-depression phase. We feel devalued and unwanted. This turns to shame and the belief that we are not good enough for their world. Uncertainty sinks in. You question your self-worth. You might go to extremes to gain acceptance, such as people pleasing or doing things for people that would ordinarily go beyond your level of acceptance.

Rejection Is about You, Not Them

One of the greatest illusions about rejection is that we convince ourselves we are being "rejected", as if someone is doing something to us. But, in fact, the rejection begins on the inside. This can be traced back to your inner critics, those old voices that tell you "You're no good," or "Why bother? You'll just fail anyway."

When we reject ourselves first, we are sending a clear message to people. It is like putting the writing on the wall yourself. People can sense when someone is lacking in confidence. If you walk into a bank to get a loan and you believe, even before you meet with the loans officer, there is no way you'll get that loan, this feeling carries with you. Be aware of situations in which you are rejecting yourself before anyone else gets a chance to.

"Each of us must confront our own fears, must come face to face with them. How we handle our fears will determine where we go with the rest of our lives. To experience adventure or to be limited by the fear of it."

The Courage to Kill Self-Rejection

What if I told you that 90 percent of the time it was you rejecting yourself instead of the world rejecting you? Would you believe me? Probably not. You would start to validate the reasons why you are rejected and make it into a real condition with all the evidence you've collected. Failures at school, relationships, or people who always say no when they should be saying yes.

We escape the risk of rejection through avoidance. We stay away from the fear of failing or looking stupid, and we miss out on so much more. We push through the fear of rejection by pushing ourselves out there, taking that risk, and trying something even if we're afraid we'll fail. By taking a risk at failing, you are gaining an important lesson—learning to accept that not everything in life is a *yes*.

The Rejection-Free Action Plan

One of the ways you fail yourself is believing that a rejection means you are worthless. Rejection happens to everyone, and if you see it as a necessary means to getting what you want rejection becomes your ally and not an enemy.

Desensitize Rejection

Desensitizing yourself to the fear of rejection is about taking action toward the events or situations that you fear the most.

Desensitization is practiced through conditioning your mind with repeated attempts at getting rejected. Based on respondent conditioning, it is a form of behavioral therapy used by psychiatrists to help people overcome deep fears and phobias. Also known as **flooding**, this type of practice can be used to condition you for rejection.

This is what you do. Make getting rejected a daily habit. Put yourself in a situation where the possibility of being rejected is high. This will break your fear of rejection by numbing it with the number of times you get told, "No."

Jia Jiang, the author of *Rejection Proof,* gives an amazing account of how he put himself out there to purposely get rejected over the course of a hundred days. You can see this on his website Rejection Therapy.com. Jiang's purpose was to get so used to being rejected that he broke all attachment to his fear about rejection. There is a lesson to be learned here: **What we repeatedly do becomes habit.**

By making rejection a daily habit, putting yourself in harm's way, you become desensitized to the emotional pain.

Are You Ready for the Challenge?

Instead of avoiding rejection, you are going to welcome it into your life. See how many situations you can create where you will possibly get rejected.

Here are ten examples:

1. In the hotel you are staying in, request to have a complimentary bottle of champagne brought up to your room.
2. Ask someone if they'd like to have a race to the end of the street.
3. Walk up to someone at random and ask if you can get your picture taken together.
4. Walk into a car dealership and ask to take an expensive car for a test-drive.
5. Go to a furniture store and ask if you can take a one-hour nap on one of their model beds.
6. Go to a local Starbucks and ask if you can work as a volunteer for the afternoon.
7. Give away a banana to 10 random people you meet on the street.
8. In a supermarket or cafe, ask if you can "skip to the front of the line" because you are "patience intolerant."
9. Check in for a flight and "ask" to be upgraded to business class (and you won't be paying extra).

10. Challenge someone to a staring contest. You have to hold the stare for a minimum of five minutes.

Stay Centered in Your Emotional Playground

What happens when your emotions are governed by the emotions of other people? When they are angry, you feel tense and nervous. If they are happy or in a good mood, you feel relaxed and at ease. By seeking that approval that rarely comes in our relationships at home or at work, we are forever being pulled back and forth.

Your emotional playground is what you can control. By staying centered in your own emotional backyard, you can own the feelings that you frequently lose touch with. For example, some kids come into your playground and they are in a bad mood. They try to disrupt things by taking control, scaring the other kids, or being hard to get along with.

Give them what they want, and they persist with the behavior. Draw the line on your boundaries and let them know they can stay as long as they behave. This is how we can monitor and maintain our emotions in almost any situation. When we fear rejection, hide our shame or try to escape, we are not centered in our own backyards. We are playing in someone else's.

It takes practice and concentration to stay aware of how you are feeling. When you feel it coming on, that's a warning sign that your fear is being triggered. You can stop this from spiraling out of control. First, say no to the loss of control. You have nothing to lose.

I have a tactic set up for this. When I am in a situation in which I feel afraid, such as when I have to speak publicly, I say to myself, "No, I'm not letting this happen." I give myself permission to have full control over what I feel and how I perform. Reacting to fears and running just keeps the cycle going.

Let Go of Past Failures That Define You

If you were rejected in the past, you'll reject yourself in the future. We replay old stories of failures and bad results from our past.

When this happens, we create more of the same. Your past is not who you are, it is who you were. Are you the same person you were twenty years ago? I know I'm not.

Sure, many parts of you haven't changed and people still refer to you as someone they know based on a lifetime of friendship. But we are all evolving even if those changes are subtle. Basing your future happiness or success on what you got in the past is a way to repeat history. You can define your future by the actions you take now. Your thoughts, words and emotions are powerful and can change your life in a moment if conditioned properly.

Build "Rejection-Free" Confidence through Practice

The way to build confidence is to take action. But doing what? Challenge yourself to do the things that are difficult. These are easy to spot because we resist what we don't want to do. We put off difficult tasks because they are hard, but they actually carry the greatest rewards in the long run.

Confidence is an "action building" activity. It can only be built when we put our fears and uncertainties to the test. You can use this list of "Rejection Strategies" as a starting point to develop a higher level of confidence and assurance.

Rewrite the Story and Break Your Fear

I want you to think about your life and the impact you would have if your fear of failure was removed. What would you start doing today? How would you respond to criticism?

Remember this if you take anything away here. You will fail at things your try for the first or second or even tenth time. You might fail in business, or a relationship, or at recovery from an addiction. But if you try hard enough and keep trying, you will succeed. The only failure that should concern you is the failure of NOT taking action.

"I do not believe in a fate that falls on men however they act; but I do believe in a fate that falls on them unless they act."

— G. K. Chesterton

Failure only defeated those people who let it win. It can only win if you decide to avoid the actions that are "risky". But the real risk is in doing nothing.

Imagine your life right now only ten years from now. You decide today to push against your resistance, break through and take action against your fear. Instead of avoiding people, you reach out and take to them. Instead of hesitating to volunteer, you're the first to step up and say, "I'll do it." Instead of procrastinating when a challenge is blocking your way, you set out right there to remove it so you can push forward.

You can break the fear of failing and live your dreams as you were meant to do. Why settle for less? Don't give in to the fears, drama, self-defeating thoughts, and negative voices of your own mind. Fight back, stay strong, breathe deeply, and make a promise to yourself: No matter what, you are here to win. No matter what, you're not giving in to the fears that tell you to play a small hand.

Never negotiate with fear. Be the master of your own fate and crush through fear with an unbreakable mindset and the resilience you are building by reading this book.

"Like success, failure is many things to many people. With Positive Mental Attitude, failure is a learning experience, a rung on the ladder, a plateau at which to get your thoughts in order and prepare to try again."

— W. Clement Stone

Breaking Bad Habits That Fuel Repetitive Failure

"The best way to stop a bad habit is to never begin it."

— **J.C. Penney**

There are three kinds of failure. There is failing fast. There is the slow-burn method and failing slowly with caution as you move forward. Next, there is the type of failure that keeps you failing without any progression at all. You just keep plodding ahead, spinning your wheels, stuck in a rut while performing the same routine over and over again expecting a different result.

This is called **repetitive failure**. It is the most common type of failing, and the most difficult to correct.

That is what happens when you continue to do the same things again and again while experiencing the same negative results. For example, you want to lose weight but you are still eating junk food twice a day. You want to watch less TV and do more reading, but every time you have free time you turn the TV on by default. Or you intend to save money but whenever you're on the computer you jump into eBay and start spending money.

This is what happens when your actions default to a string of bad habits. In the moment, something as innocent as clicking that buy button does not feel like such a big deal. You just spent $10.00. But if you clicked that same button once a day, again and again, for 365 consecutive days, you would have spent close to $4000 in a year. You know how fast a year goes by, right? How about ten years? Your habit is failing your financial goals.

Have you been failing to lose that fat percentage and get into the best shape ever? I struggled with this for years. I went to the gym often and exercised when I felt like it (that is a bad habit too). But when I watched TV at night, I found myself with an ice cream in one hand and peanuts in the other. My habit of eating junk was defeating my desire to get into great shape.

What habits do you act on every day that defeat you? I'll bet you have at least one, and you know what it is. Now, before you beat yourself up over this, realize that habits are reversible. They are not easy to implement, but over time, you will be able to change your bad habits by practicing better ones.

Bad Habits on Autopilot

What we have here are a group of habits that are operating on autopilot because we haven't organized and built a new system to stop them. Now, I am not saying you have to give up television or junk food, but if gaining weight is causing your health to fail and you have a desire to turn this around and don't, you will continue to experience weight gain. This tells your brain that you are fat, lazy and lack the discipline to change. This equals failure.

By failing to stop spending, you fail to save anything. By failing to put an end to junk food consumption, you fail to lose weight. By failing to control your impulsive television watching, you fail to read more books. This results in double failure because you also fail to better your knowledge and improve yourself.

Repetitive failure is fueled by a system of bad habits that have been failing you for years. Some of these habits appear to happen so naturally that we just accept them even when they harm us. Habits, when left to control your actions, act as the lead that pulls you here and there. It would appear you have no control over your desires, cravings or sudden impulses. But, in fact, you are still making choices, if at a subconscious level, as in not thinking about the next step but just doing it.

Getting back to the issue of someone who wants to lose weight yet every evening, at approximately 8:00 p.m., she goes to the fridge and gets an ice cream. Then that is followed by a bag of chips.

Your failure point is you never have money you can't figure out. You have a job and get paid twice a month. Yet by Monday you're broke. What happened? Every Saturday you are in the habit of going to the races or casino. Or you shop online and have the "Buy Now" addiction. By Sunday night you are empty again. You failed yourself again, but the repetitive failure continues...

Until...

You need an intervention of your bad habits. So much of our wins from day to day fall on the habits we acquire throughout our lifetime. Everyone has a system of habits that they perform every minute of the day, but only a select few influence your life on a massive scale. Surprisingly, your system of bad habits is not difficult to overcome. If they are, it is because your mind has convinced you they are.

The mind likes to have its way. In fact, it wants to do everything its way. It does what it wants and makes decisions in the moment driven by the thought of, *I want...* or, *I need...* and this triggers your compulsion.

There is very little your mind needs that is going to kill you if you go without it. When you deny your mind what it wants, it resorts to manipulation, convincing you that, *This is the last time,* or, *Just one more (purchase, donut, game) isn't going to hurt you.* But...

We are aware of the game now. You have been focusing on the impulsive drive of your desires in the moment. Looking at the big picture and visualizing your success at the end of 60 days is going to give you the motivation and courage to say, "NO." Saying no to your own desires feels like self-deprivation (another trick the mind likes to play), but the truth is you are depriving yourself of a greater reward when you say, "YES," to the moment.

Never believe for a moment that by giving in to your impulsive needs you are fulfilling your desires and therefore getting ahead. It is always the reverse. The world might fail you in many ways, but it could never amount to the failure you bring upon yourself.

The failure to reach your goals, the failure to succeed at the passions driving you, is always an inside job. You fail first in your mind, your thoughts support this failure, and then that failure is final when your default actions complete the circuit.

How can you break your bad habits that are failing you, interrupt the pattern, and turn your fails into wins?

Identify the bad habits that are causing you to fail. If you're not changing, or you feel stuck, is it a pattern that you have failed to recognize? One strategy I started doing was making notes as I worked through my day. I would wake up and start doing stuff, and as I moved through the day, I would make notes about what I was doing.

Where was I wasting time? What was I procrastinating on? How much TV did I watch? What goals did I not hit for the day and why?

Monitoring your actions doesn't sound like an exciting activity to do, but you don't have to do this every day. Track your habits by being aware of what you focus on. Many of our habits are ingrained. We don't see what's working and what is not.

For example, one habit I had never recognized until recently was waking up, sitting down at the computer, and diving right into email at 5:00 a.m. This is a mindless, exhausting time suck that is highly unproductive. I realized that by stopping this habit, I was able to focus on writing first thing in the morning.

When you stop a bad habit, you have to replace it with another one. Your new habit is a refined, high-quality activity that adds value to your purpose and your day.

It takes decades of practice to master your bad habits. It doesn't take this long to undo your bad habits and create positive, high-octane habits that fill you with energy. Bad habits are draining, but a system of good habits supported by a disciplined routine can defeat the habits holding you back. Many of us have been living with our old habits for so long that we don't recognize them as the reason behind internal failure.

You can't always see the enemy that sleeps in your house. When it comes to habits and behavior, we need to take a step outside of ourselves to recognize the pattern of self-defeat that exists underneath the surface of our actions. This is where limiting behavior and the bad habits supporting it exist.

Habit Switching: A System to Prevent Habit Failure

Here I am giving you a system for habit change. There will be challenges with this as you try to plug your bad habit and replace it with something else. As your willpower struggles with the change, for the first few weeks you can expect to feel like someone going through withdrawal. When you've built lifelong habits that stick, changing your behavior results in resistance. The stronger you push, the stronger the resistance, until you win over and push right through.

Consider a few things before you start. First of all, not every habit needs to be corrected. The bad habits I focused on to start with were impacting my daily life, work and relationships.

Identify Your "Negative Triggers"

If your bad habit is checking your email first thing in the morning, this habitual act is hardwired into your psyche. I would wake up at 5:00 a.m. with every intention to be productive with writing, exercise and meditation—and before I knew it I was on the computer. I had to identify the trigger. It was not being prepared. As soon as I opened my laptop, this became an automatic response. I was laser focused on the wrong task.

My friend was in the habit of stopping by the same bar almost every night for a quick one. This led to him getting home later, usually $40 short of cash, and less time with family. He tried to stop, but five nights a week he found himself going out after work.

When I asked him what compelled his choices, he said, "I can't help it; the place is on my way home." The trigger was obvious. If he was in the vicinity of this bar, he dropped in after work, at a time of day when his willpower was at an all-time low.

How did he break this habit? First, he took a different route home. This removed the first trigger. Then, at the end of the day, he paid himself $40, the equivalent of what he was spending a night in this place. This provided proof that there was a heavy cost in his stopping into this place every night.

Adapt an Understanding of Willpower

Willpower, by the way, doesn't work when it comes to shifting your habits. You start the day with a full tank, but as your willpower becomes depleted throughout the day, your resistance shrinks. Something you'd normally say no to, you might say yes to when willpower levels are weak.

Many people who try to switch habits do really well during the day—when they are feeling mentally and physically strong—but after putting in ten hours a day, dangle a chocolate bar or cigarette in front of them and they'll snatch it up right away. We are, after all, only human.

Set Realistic Goals

Let's say our decision is to create a habit of reading more books. This would increase your knowledge and would be a better activity than watching TV. If you stick with thirty minutes of reading per day, you could read five books in a month. But if thirty minutes is a tough habit to stick with, try just ten minutes a day. This is easily manageable.

In fact, most habits could be built in just five to ten minutes per day. You don't have to invest an hour every day or push yourself to the brink of exhaustion.

Break it down into small chunks and you'll have created your new habit within thirty days. You want to write a book? Start with a hundred words per day. You want to wake up earlier? Start by setting your alarm ten minutes earlier. You could also build a habit to go to bed earlier. Remember it's not the big result that we're going for but building the behavior. Once you master the routine, you can scale up at any time.

Focus on Habit Replacement, Not Habit Elimination

When it comes to building new habits, our initial thought is, *I have to eliminate the old habits.* If you want to eat healthier to lose weight and get into better shape, eliminating junk food intake isn't a realistic plan. Instead, focus on reducing the habit a little bit every week.

Reduce your sugar intake every day by ten percent. You'll have less pressure to do it perfectly. You can apply this to any habit you are attempting to break. Want to reduce the amount of time you spend online? Start cutting down by five percent a day. You can set up blocks of time when you're offline altogether instead of wired to your cellphone or computer.

To get away from constantly looking at your cell phone, consider buying a regular alarm clock and a watch. This will prevent you from using your phone as an alarm and keep you from looking at it as soon as you wake up. Now that you have a watch, you won't need to check your phone for the time—which means you won't get distracted by other notifications on your screen either.

Action Plan:

Reduce your habits by five percent a day. Don't simply eliminate. Then you can hit your goals much more realistically. Focus on reduction, not elimination.

Focus on Long-Term Conversion

It takes time to change a habit. About 60 days, to be exact.

According to a <u>study released in the European Study of Social Psychology</u>, a team of researchers led by Phillippa Lally surveyed ninety-six people over twelve weeks to reveal how long it took to develop a new habit. At the end of the survey, Lally analyzed the results of the experiment and determined the time it took to form a new habit was approximately sixty-six days.

We need long-term focus and consistent concentration over a period of months to make it happen. If you are expecting to see massive gains after two weeks, you could be setting yourself up to fail. Think long-term habit change and stay focused on your daily repetitions.

For example, an area I had been failing in for years is exercising consistently. I would always have a short workout randomly when I was motivated. I couldn't commit to the 60 minutes a day. So, I started by stretching for ten minutes a day. Then I added push-ups into the routine.

From there I built it up to one set of arm curls. I continued to do this for 30–40 days, never missing a day. On the days I resisted, I would remind myself of my why, and this would propel me to do it. Your why is big leverage. Don't underestimate this.

By the end of the month I no longer needed reminders. This routine was becoming part of my regular daily activity. If I missed a day (and I did) I would feel it.

Action Plan:

Have a long-term focus and scale up slowly. Whatever your habit, you can achieve your goal by scaling slowly. Stay fixed on the behaviour.

Keep it simple. Focus on one habit at a time.

Habit building doesn't have to be complicated. You can keep it simple by trying the following:

- Focus on one habit a time.

- Perform the same action every day.

- Perform this action at the same time every day.

- Scale up gradually.

- Measure your results.

The nature of any habit is repetition. The force of that habit is decided by the results you get from the action. If you have a bad habit or an addiction such as gambling, your reward is the euphoric high you feel when you win. But the result is that you could lose all your money.

A better habit would be to invest your money. While you may not see the return on your investment as quickly as you would from winning a game, over time you'll be rewarded. The nature of your success depends on the habits you feed.

Motivating Factors

To make any habit shift, you need to be motivated to change. What is the outcome you're wanting to achieve? What actions do you have to take each day to achieve this? What will be the downfall if you fail to break this habit?

This is why you need a primary motivating factor. It is a compelling reason so strong that it drives you to build your new habit into your daily life.

For example, John was in the habit of watching TV for two to three hours a day. He knew this was highly unproductive, but when he got home from work, he didn't feel like doing anything else. He had a dream to create his own online business selling training courses that he created.

John worked in a day job that was sucking all his energy and so, at the end of the day, he just wanted to chill out and do nothing. Short term, he was using the TV to escape from his present reality. But long term, this habit was stealing his dream and keeping him stuck in TV land with no hope of change.

John recognized this as damaging to the quality of his life. Three hours of TV a day, 20 hours a week, and over 80 hours a month meant that he could build his business in six months.

What did he do? John stopped television during the week and worked on his dream by waking up 90 minutes earlier in the morning. During the day, instead of spending his lunch hour surfing the net or playing with his smartphone, he found a place to work and put in one more hour. At night, he would do another hour before winding down before bed.

John's prime motivator was quitting his day job and totally revamping the quality of his lifestyle by doing the work he loved. And he did it by:

1. creating a vision for what he wanted.

2. making a habit shift fueled by his primary motivation.

You can have anything you want if your motivational factor is strong enough. One more critical element to consider is *what is your main distractor?* This is the one thing that could derail you from changing your habit. This could be a trigger that draws you back into the habit, and it happens so subtly you don't realize it until it's too late. For example, working on a book and you constantly get distracted by the internet, so you end up short on your written word count.

My main distractor that derailed my "writing habit" in the morning was the habit of checking email as soon as I sat down at my desk to write. It was a built-in habit by default. Once I started I couldn't stop until I went through everything. But this would steal away an hour and then the time was gone.

I used Post-it notes as reminders and tacked these up on my computer and on my desk: "No email until writing is complete."

I had to break the pattern. Occasionally I'd be writing and suddenly find myself in my inbox responding to email that I had declared as "urgent." It was a reaction that took time and effort to change, but, gradually, I was able to sit for one hour without being distracted by email or notifications.

Ask yourself: *What is my primary distractor?*

> *"In reading the lives of great men, I found that the first victory they won was over themselves...self-discipline with all of them came first."*
>
> **— Harry S. Truman**

Test Your Habits

You won't know right away if your replacement habit is working. You need to give it a chance. The best way to know if it's working is to check in with how you feel after completing your new habit routine.

In John's case, the reward at the end of the day was to see the work he was getting done on his business. Watching television produced nothing, but after one week of working on his training courses, he had already completed several modules. The progress filled him with enthusiasm and watching television every night ceased to become a challenge.

Your habits can make or break you. People fail from bad habits more than from anything else. Sometimes all it takes is breaking one bad habit and you can change everything.

Bad habits are never easy because, even though it might be stealing your time (excessive TV watching or surfing the net) or putting on weight (eating junk food every night) there is a reward your mind and body craves. To break the habit, you need to introduce a new reward system.

In the case of John, his reward from watching TV was that he could relax and get rid of stress. But, in fact, it was costing him his dream. Once he established a new reward system, this was strong enough to override the previous reward he would feel watching television all night.

Habit Reminders

It takes approximately 66 days for a habit to be fully integrated, according to Phillippa Lally, a health psychology researcher at University College London. She based her research on a **study on habits** published in the *European Journal of Social Psychology*.

This means you'll need to be diligent during this timeframe if you want to succeed. But what I experienced is that, after 14 days, I had gained considerable momentum in my work. I used a system of habit reminders as well as tracking progress, so I could identify the reward at the end of the day.

So, a strategy that works is to set up habit reminders around your room. You can write these reminders down in your daily journal or on a wall calendar like I do. You want to create an alert for the replacement habit. You can use app alerts such as **HabitTimer** or **Task Reminder**. These apps send you an alert when it is time to be working on your replacement habit. I use the alarm on my phone to go off at the same time every morning when I am supposed to be working on my project.

Now, here are three effective strategies you can use to make sure you stick with replacing your bad habits:

Commit to Working Toward Your Plan

A calendar or schedule book would be convenient at this stage. I use a wall calendar to plan my week and my tasks. This is a great form of self-discipline: Getting organized!

Now that you have a list of actions, ordered by priority, you can start penciling in the steps on a calendar. The calendar will serve as a reminder of the actions you are focusing on.

Once you know what to do, it is a matter of committing to it. Know what you have to do, commit yourself to the plan, and then…

Follow through with Consistent Action

Get busy. Once you commit to your plan, stick with it. The longer you work the action steps and move closer to achieving your goals, the more you will have defeated the path of least resistance. It isn't enough just to do something every now and then and expect to improve. It has to be consistent. Work until it's finished.

Consistency is the key to molding a habit. The actions you fix your focus on over a long period of time determine the results you accomplish. By devoting 10 to 20 minutes a day toward mastering a specific skill set, you can set this habit on autopilot after 60 days.

Implement the Seinfeld strategy and use a wall calendar to mark an "action taken" for each day. If you exercise that day, put a check on the calendar for that day. But miss a day and nothing gets checked. Don't break the chain method, which builds consistency.

Take Daily Inventory

Before going to sleep, take a few minutes to review your day. Look at the problems, challenges, and situations you faced and make mental notes on the methods you used to deal with these challenges. How could you have reacted differently? Was the problem resolved or is it still unfinished?

Take a look at your interactions with people and come up with ideas you can use to improve your communication with them. Make this step a daily habit! This is one of the most important exercises you will do because it is a great way to clean your slate. It will provide you with some perspective as to how you deal with situations and where your weaknesses are in relation to your strengths.

"Any fact facing us is not as important as our attitude toward it, for that determines our success or failure. The way you think about a fact may defeat you before you ever do anything about it. You are overcome by the fact because you think you are."

— **Norman Vincent Peale**

The Stopping Power of Past Failure

"What matters is this: being fearless of failure arms you to break the rules. In doing so, you may change the culture and just possibly, for a moment, change life itself."

— **Malcolm Mclaren**

Your past history of failing can be a hindrance to your future success and damage the quality of life you could be experiencing. The past has a strong influence on how you are living in the now.

Many people, and this might be you, are using the past as a measuring stick for creating future success. But as you will see, your past does not equal your future. You have failed most of your life? Good for you. Now you have the courage to pick up today and do what you were born to do: win big!

Before I go any further, I want you to visualize something. Imagine you are in a race and the other runners are ahead of you, running fast towards the finish line. You try to keep up, but no matter how hard you push to get ahead, you fail to pick up any momentum.

You don't know what the problem is but your heart and mind feel heavy with strong negative emotions. You feel strong resentment towards the other runners because they are stronger, faster, and are obviously going to reach the finish line before you.

One of the runners that were in the lead suddenly takes a fall. He stumbles over his shoelaces and hits the pavement hard, scraping his legs and is in immeasurable pain. You think to yourself, "Okay, good, he's done. One less person I have to beat." But as you have this sudden thought, your speed slows down even more. You almost feel sick inside at just thinking this.

202 · SCOTT ALLAN

That is when you notice it. In that moment, you can see, for the first time, what is happening to you and what has been happening, not just during this race, but in the race of life.

You look down at your ankle and can see a heavy chain there trailing back to a large, massive ball. You realize—for the first time—the truth about your life's failures. The primary reason you could never succeed is that you have been carrying this heavy burden with you the whole time. As you look closer, you can see this massive ball has stitched to its surface "Not going anywhere."

This massive ball represents your past failures, and the weight you are carrying is all your resentment, bitterness, envy, blind ambition, rationalization, and fear. The ball represents everything holding you back. You can see the negative consequences of carrying this heavy burden with you. It has turned you hard, callous, and competitive. But as competitive as you are, you never win.

Now, if you are this runner, what would you do? I know what I'd do. I would reach down and break that chain. I would ask for the freedom to live again, to be rid of the attachment of past trauma and negative thoughts holding me prisoner.

With that, you reach out with your mind and break the chain with your thoughts. You say to yourself, "I am not the past. I am the NOW. I acknowledge all my pain and let it go. I am free."

As you do this, instead of running ahead to try and win the race, you stop to help the fallen runner up. Other runners are whipping past you but you don't notice. You are not the same person you were five minutes ago, carrying around the weight of the universe filled with emotional baggage.

In cutting away the pain of past failings, you become free.

Reliving Your Negative Experience

If you were to ask someone, "Would you like to spend time in prison?" they would naturally laugh at you as if to say, "Are you crazy? Spend my days locked up, unable to move around, without the freedom of doing what I love to do?"

Yet, this is how most people live out their lives—trapped in the prison of their own mind, reliving out past events, still looking for absolution, forgiveness. Weighed down in regret, we swim around in the darkness of the mind looking for a way out. But all doors are locked. Buried underneath the bitterness, resentment, and negative thoughts of the past, you struggle day by day to find any joy or fulfillment.

Your negative experiences of the past mistakes and failures continue to play a role in your life. You try something new for the first time, but as soon as you don't get a successful result, you quit. Or an opportunity to make a change in your life is presented to you, and the fear of not succeeding makes you pass it up.

I have seen people throw away countless opportunities to change or make a difference, and they turned away, going back to doing the same old thing even though they were miserable. Your misery becomes so comfortable that, after a while, it is the only thing you know. And then, to support this, we seek out others just as stuck as we are.

In playing the victim role, we become victims of our own tragic past failings. But look at what some successful people have overcome: tragedy, loss, and failure beyond anything many of us have ever or will ever experience. And yet, they pushed forward, persevered, pushed through resistance and, without letting the tragedy define who they are, achieved a massive breakthrough.

As long as you are stuck in the failings of your past, you become the slowest runner in the race, unable to make it to the finish line with all of your baggage towing behind you.

Forget about winning because you won't even come in last. If your setbacks from the past are holding you back, we must break through these obstacles by owning them. When you take ownership of the past, the future belongs to you.

To move ahead today, you must be ready to let go of your past mistakes and failures. All of it is necessary to bring you up to this point in your life. Even if you're not where you wanted to be right now, you can push ahead and fail forward at any time. You are not a failure but someone who lives to fail so you can fail faster and build that forward momentum.

> *"Don't dwell on what went wrong. Instead, focus on what to do next.*
> *Spend your energies on moving forward*
> *toward finding the answer."*

— Denis Waitley

Letting Go of Your Baggage: Resentment and Regret

There are two forms of damaging negative emotions that tie your mind to the past. The first is resentment, that feeling of deep internal anger directed towards a person or event for a wrong that caused you emotional stress and damage. The second is regret, that deep-seated feeling of never having achieved the success you wanted.

Your mind creates what it focuses on. If your thoughts are fixated on your shortcomings of yesterday, and you dwell on these past mistakes as failures that should never have been, you will be caught in a loop of negative regret. You can't change what happened, and yet, you feel obligated to fixate on this event in your life as a huge minus.

You might say something like, "If only I hadn't lost that money ten years ago, I wouldn't be here today." The mind focused on the baggage of the past creates more of the same kind of failure…in the present. This spills over into the future.

When you relive the past, you sacrifice the present and destroy the future.

You need a new perspective and a better way to look at your past events as stepping stones to greater things. Because that is exactly what they are. All your mishaps, problems, and struggles throughout life have led to here. More importantly, your attitude towards past events has either moved you ahead…or is keeping you trapped.

The past is a playground of learning, experience and growth. Everything that you experience becomes your story. Many people see their past failures as just that—mistakes that they continue to dwell on and regret. Regret becomes resentment, and this leads to negative emotions that corrupt opportunities and infect your dreams.

Release Your Resentment

Resentment is a form of negative energy that eats away at us over time, leading to depression, anxiety, and other negative emotions.

These resentments are the judgments and perceptions formed about other people, places, or events that have wronged, harmed, or victimized us, as perceived by the ego-mind. Just because you are angry about something, doesn't necessarily mean you are right about it.

You might have a good reason for your bitterness: a case of dishonesty, theft, abuse, or something said or done that caused you some form of emotional, physical, or mental harm. You have latched onto this pain and are refusing to give in or let go. Years later, the anger and bitterness have turned against you, transforming into your worst enemy.

Taking on resentment is like swallowing a bitter pill. You are linking the pain and suffering of the past to the thoughts and emotions of the present. Bitter, deep-seated anger and resentment builds over the years.

Some people hold onto deep grudges as if it brings some kind of relief to remember what was done to them by someone who betrayed their trust.

When you resent someone or something, you are invariably handing over your power to that person or situation. A mentor once said to me, "The definition of suffering is being bitter toward someone and having him or her be completely unaware of it."

While you are busy wasting your creative thoughts and energy on people you don't like for whatever reason, they are living their lives elsewhere, completely oblivious to your anger.

Do yourself a favor and find a way to get over the pain caused by past events. I am not suggesting that you try to forget these painful events, but how you choose to deal with them is entirely up to you. The grief you're holding onto is your responsibility. It is time to let go, move on, and live your life.

Take an Inventory of Your Resentment

I created a "resentment inventory" and included the names of the people and events I resented as well as the reason behind my resentment. Here are six steps to help you prepare your resentment inventory:

- Create a list. Make a list of all the people, places, events, and/or principles that you resent. Write down the names of all the people and places and details of the events.

- List the causes. Now, go back to the top of the list and in another column or on a separate piece of paper, write down the cause of the resentment for each item. Why are you angry? What happened?

- How has this resentment affected you? Next, write down how each event affected you. Did it impact your wealth, self-esteem, emotional state, or security?

- What is the benefit of holding on? Most people feel they are gaining something by resenting the source of their pain. Write down what you are gaining from continuing to hold onto your resentment.

- What is your role in this situation? As someone who has been wronged, you might think you are the victim, and therefore, take no responsibility. However, what thoughts are you harboring that feed into this? How do you continue to hand over your personal power to the source of your resentment?

Regret is a Decision

Regret that is not dealt with or accepted eats away at you over time. You end up feeling as if you are constantly living with the ghosts of your past, forever haunted by memories of events that can never be changed. When you hold onto regrets, you are living in an illusion and clinging to false hopes.

Identifying things in your life for which you are grateful is an effective way to deal with regret. There may have been a different outcome had you done things differently, but how do you know it would have been better?

The choices and decisions you make at any given moment are based on who you are at that time. You did what you felt was right. You will do what you feel needs to be done today based on who you are right now and the information you possess to make those choices.

Here is a list of regrets you might be holding onto:

- Not taking a chance on your dreams

- Passing on opportunities to change your job

- Too much time wasted on thoughts of worry and fear

- Never doing anything bold or adventurous

- Spending all your money instead of investing it

- Not enough time spent with your children.

If you do have regrets—a job you lost, a relationship that didn't work out, or a decision you made that ended badly—would your life be different if everything had worked out according to plan? Is everything in life supposed to work out perfectly?

I was once told that regret, although very real, is an illusion of the worst kind. It is a false belief that convinces you that all your choices and past experiences have failed you. This simply isn't true. You had certain expectations that were never met, and when the outcome you desperately wanted failed to come true, you feel regretful.

You have a choice to stay stuck in your regret and self-pity. Nothing is holding you there. You are the master of your own mind. If regret, resentment and self-pity are what you are stuck on, you can change this at any moment. This is your reality, and you have the freedom to create it as you like.

Life is made up of wins and losses. For some people, they lose a lot more than they win. But the winners are the people who charge forward when they get knocked down over and over again. They don't stop for pity or to make excuses.

Banish your regret and count your gratitude. That is your choice. You get to choose how you view your circumstances.

Staying Grounded in the Present

Living in the past with the hope of changing it, or wishing it'd been different somehow, puts a cripple on the future. You can't have both worlds. You need to choose one.

As long as you are hanging out with the ghosts of the past, you will never move on. If you are locked into an abysmal state of nostalgic fantasy, you cannot focus on the only period of your life that really matters—the present.

The haunts of the past are with you and may always be, but they don't have to control your future. You can control the tendency to relive the past by awakening to the notion that you have choices in every moment of every day, and how you choose to live each day is up to you.

There is nothing wrong with telling tales of the past or thinking about past events. Everyone has a past. Everyone has a story to tell that is unique to that person, and they are shaped and molded by their past.

When your present mind exists in the past, it becomes lost in mirrors of disillusionment. Instead of creating a better future, you recreate the history of past events without a future. When this happens, the past is never finished so long as it is kept alive by the reminder of past regrets and failures.

"You build on failure. You use it as a stepping stone. Close the door on the past. You don't try to forget the mistakes, but you don't dwell on it. You don't let it have any of your energy, or any of your time, or any of your space."

— Johnny Cash

Think of the past as much as you need to and use it to your advantage as a measuring stick to remind yourself of how far you have come and how much you have grown. If it's used as a form of punishment, the pain of self-loathing can turn into a destructive force.

Free yourself by living in the present. This will help you break the habit and lose the mental attraction to return to past memories.

By relinquishing your connection with the past deeds and outcomes that cannot be altered, you seek to create new opportunities and increase your chances of achieving success. Instead of recreating and reliving the past, you open up higher realms of thought. This expands to creating a greater positive outflow of energy and helps you find fulfillment.

Forgiveness is a positive step toward releasing the pain that you've been holding onto. You don't have to forget what has happened, but by undertaking the courageous act of forgiving someone, you are giving yourself and the other person the permission to move on, to let go, and to heal.

Forgiving extricates you from playing the role of a weak victim and empowers you to take the path of the courageous.

Failing Fast in Motion

Create a list of the events, memories, and past failures holding you back. Be 100% honest and dive deep into your fears to discover what is failing you now. Until you can move on from this, you will have to bear your own "ball and chain" until you decide to cut it loose.

Once you have identified what is keeping you prisoner, use this process to set your past free:

1. Acknowledge your role in this situation.

2. Forgive the people that harmed you.

3. Forgive yourself for the harm you did to others,

4. Practice deep breathing for five minutes. As you breathe in for four seconds, you draw the past into your body and acknowledge it. Breathing out (exhaling), you let it go.

5. Work this process until your past becomes a memory that you no longer become trapped in.

Self-Compassion and the Gift of Failing

"Compassion isn't some kind of self-improvement project or ideal that we're trying to live up to. Having compassion starts and ends with having compassion for all those unwanted parts of ourselves, all those imperfections that we don't even want to look at."

— Pema Chodron,
American Tibetan Buddhist and author of
When Things Fall Apart

In the ground-breaking book, *Reinventing Your Life*, authors Dr. Jeffrey E. Young and Dr. Janet S. Klosko, refer to a term they coined empathic self-confrontation. In the book, the authors state:

"Show compassion for yourself, while continually pushing yourself to change. Many people either criticize themselves too harshly when they do not feel they have changed enough, or they are too lenient and make excuses to let themselves off the hook. The process of change is very difficult. Above all, be compassionate with yourself. You are struggling to do your best. Be understanding of your limitations and flaws."

As we have discussed throughout this book, many of our struggles with handling failures branch out from our ability to structuralize the negative experiences attached to mistakes, failures and internal disappointment. You might be used to hammering on yourself for not being good enough. Being kind to yourself could be an experience you are not yet familiar with. Your mind could still be stuck on the pains of your past and blaming someone —your parents, an old relationship, or former boss—for your failures in life.

A part of the *Fail Big* formula is developing a deeper sense of self through loving-kindness and self-compassion. What does compassion have to do with failing fast and becoming a champ at learning to fail? Isn't this book designed to make me tougher, resilient, and full of grit?

Yes, and that is why you need a clear understanding of how compassion—for yourself and other fellows—is the true path to living successfully. The "soul" purpose of this journey isn't about becoming successful but rather, learning to live successfully. In order to do this, self-compassion plays a critical role. Imagine what you could accomplish, where you could go, and who you could become if you had a level of compassion for yourself so deep that nothing could break it.

When you love who you are at the highest level, you will never fear failing again. You will form the thoughts of forgiveness, not for the mistakes you've made in the past, but you will practice the art of forgiving yourself for these mistakes. Your compassion for YOU is the driving force behind why failing is such a positive event and not the negative monster that is to be feared. When you love and let go of this fear, you invite the gift of failing into your life.

Self-compassion ties everything together. When you can embrace that deeper love for who you are, your mission, and the importance you bring to this world, compassion begins with clarity of your mindful intent. If failing has always been your fear, the solution to breaking this fear is self-kindness. You are on this path to fail with happiness. To fail knowing you are cared for. To fail knowing there is no failure, but lessons learned on a never-ending journey of continuous growth and self-improvement.

Owning the responsibility to change is the greatest gift you can give yourself. It is the greatest sense of self-compassion there is— to forgive yourself in times of turmoil. You are pushing hard to change, and it isn't an easy path. This is why many people fail to begin with. They are expecting an easy conversion. If it were easy, we would all be healthy, well-balanced people. Know your flaws and be willing to focus on adjusting as you grow. It is one step at a time, and one day at a time.

*"When you say 'Yes' to others, make sure you are not
saying 'No' to yourself."*

— Paulo Cohelo

Self-Compassion is an Act of Surrender

One of the difficulties in giving into self-compassion is giving up the trap of childhood fears and securities. There are memories, emotions and attachments that keep you glued to your past because that is a place of comfortability, even if it hurts to stay there.

We feel safe when shrouded in the safety of old patterns, even though they can be emotionally damaging in the long-term. You want to be sure that you are not clinging to old limiting beliefs trapping you from moving ahead or merging into a new way of life free from the fears of failure.

Be certain your thoughts and actions are guiding you in the right direction. Surrender to the faith that you are on a journey of incredible circumstances and that, not everyone gets this chance. You have been handed a gift, and now you have to open it to see what is inside.

If you're looking for validation that you're okay, how about this: you made it. You're here. We are on this page together discussing the joys of living and the happiness that comes with being kind to yourself in a gentle, understanding way. You can now look yourself in the mirror and say, "Here I am. I did it!" You have survived this journey and now you can thrive for the rest of it

Gary Vaynerchuk says, *"The odds of becoming a human are 400 trillion to 1."* If this is true, time is too short to not live each day to its maximum. You have limited time on this planet, and one life to live, and this life is happening right now.

The greatest gift anyone can receive is from the heart, and as you heal from the patterns of your past, push self-defeat aside to make space for new relationships, and a new way of living that only

214 · SCOTT ALLAN

failing big can bring you. This is the essence of surrendering to a bigger vision for yourself.

Everyone is broken to some extent, but that is where your strength can be found. I like what Ernest Hemmingway said: *"The world breaks everyone, and afterward, some are strong at the broken places."*

As we learn to accept ourselves as flawed human beings on a spiritual journey, it becomes a simpler process of self-acceptance. You are not meant to be perfect in all the things you do, but the perfection is doing these things with failed intention. You may try and not succeed, but you keep trying, and without fail, you will move past the broken patterns of denial and self-delusion.

We carry so much weight around that has been hanging on to our hearts and minds for years: failures that you hold onto, the voices of criticism speaking lies about your shortcomings, and flaws that formed as character defects. Your self-compassion begins with forgiveness. This is the place for empathic confrontation, as you push yourself to change, without adding any deadlines or pressure to achieve a certain level of success.

You have made many mistakes on this journey, and hopefully, your failings are viewed as stepping stones to the greatness of who you are becoming. To fail is to move forward. To be self-compassionate is doing what you love to do. It is saying NO to people when you must, without feeling guilty for it. It is taking time out to exist as you are by stepping out of the "race" and giving time to reflect. Your self-compassion is grounded in the time you spend doing what you love to do with the people you love to do it with.

Tara Brach, the author of *Radical Acceptance*, has said:

"Feeling compassion for ourselves in no way releases us from responsibility for our actions. Rather, it releases us from the self-hatred that prevents us from responding to our life with clarity and balance."

Life is Flawed, Fragile and Filled with Suffering

Let's look at failure from a different perspective. There are many ways humans fail throughout life as we strive for a better way to do things, a better way to live. But what about a failed human? Someone who lives in poverty, has made all the wrong choices, living on the streets, housed up in a crack house and their days filled with drug use.

A human that has given up on life and whose suffering goes far beyond anything you might have experienced. We know these people because they are all around you. If you can't see the suffering of the many, you are ignoring the calling of the helpless and the needy. How do you react when you meet or see someone that is down and out on life? Do you feel pity, sympathy, empathy, or repulsion?

Compassion involves seeing and recognizing the suffering in all human beings. You actually stop for a moment to observe this person's pain, their failure in life. You absorb the suffering of people by thinking for a time about their situation and the pain they are going through.

Self-compassion is grounded in holding yourself responsible. You can no longer blame or hold a grudge against the people who wronged or hurt you. It is the buildup of this resentment that destroys your peace of mind. If you want to be unkind to yourself, walk around with hate in your heart and mind. It is a terrible form of mental illness that you create for yourself. Remember, you are always in control of the madness that fills up your mind.

The next time you are feeding into your victim mentality, you can stop yourself and flip it around. Refuse to go there. Refuse to be the victim anymore. This is self-empowerment. This is you taking a stand and saying NO to the negative emotions that rise up to destroy you.

Now you have the tools and the know-how. You have the courage and the wisdom. You have the answers, and sometimes you don't have the answers, and it's okay to admit this. What matters is that you end the verbal and mental abuse targeted towards the one person you should love the most...yourself. I say this in a non-egotistical way. Failing to love and accept yourself sets you up for failing in other areas where self-care is a priority. If you fail to care for YOU, it is difficult to express this true compassion for anyone else.

A friend once said to me, "I don't care about myself. My children are all that matter." I totally get that, but what will happen when your kids are grown up and leave you, what will you be left with? There will be a big empty hole in your life that you'll try to fill up with something or somebody else.

Of course, we love our kids, parents, and friends and you want to care for them. But think about how much bigger that love can be when you start the self-compassion with yourself. Besides, if you are leaning on others to be fulfilled, this turns into empty co-dependence. Love begins with self-compassion, and like a spider's web, it branches out to everyone from there. People will be attracted to you because you radiate this from within.

> *"When you begin to touch your heart or let your heart be touched, you begin to discover that it's bottomless, that it doesn't have any resolution, that this heart is huge, vast, and limitless. You begin to discover how much warmth and gentleness is there, as well as how much space."*

> — **PEMA CHÖDRÖN**, author of
> *Welcoming the Unwelcome*

As the Buddhists have been teaching for centuries, compassion begins with the self. It's from this place of self-compassion that genuine love extends into the mind and heart. It is fully recognizing your human journey and the gifts you carry with you to share with the world.

There are no more grudges—not just against others—all resentment, criticism and judgment melts away when you enter into this place. It involves seeing suffering and recognizing it as our shared human condition.

Another reason self-compassion truly matters is because failing—when perceived as a negative event—becomes a form of suffering. You use negative language towards yourself, act highly self-critical, and the bigger the failures, the worse it is. That sense of hopelessness sinks in over the years and you lose passion and dreams die away. When your dreams die, what else is there?

Focusing on self-compassion brings all of this back. No matter whom you are right now—a homeless person on the street or the CEO of a large corporation—these parallels don't matter. I have seen homeless people help others and people with power and everything in their grasp use this power for their own benefit. When you lose the gift of kindness and ignore the suffering of others, you are on a path of failing that only compassion can regenerate.

It's always your choice.

Here are two exercises to building a deeper relationship with yourself and others. You can focus on performing one exercise every week. When you feel yourself moving into that deeper place of self-compassion, try another activity. These practices are a mix of meditation, mindfulness, and breathing.

Be prepared to get uncomfortable. But hey, you are to make a difference and tap into your heart and mind. This path is the beginning of that journey. You are now going to focus on what Kristin Neff calls "Ending the madness".

Shift Your Critical Self-Talk

There is a monster inside of you, and it tears you apart with every chance it gets. This critical monster has grown very strong over the years, and as you may have noticed, it is difficult to control. This is your internal critic that unleashes rants of demoralizing words and it appears to happen so naturally, you rarely notice it when it is taking place. But when you mess up or fail big time, it's there to remind you of your failure.

It sounds like this:

- "Now you've gone and done it!"

- "Now look at this. You think you're going to succeed if you can't do this one simple thing?"

The first step to turning down your internal noise is awareness that it's there. Just acknowledge its presence when it begins throwing insults at you. There is a double-throw to this process, however. If your critical monster can't get to you, it will try to get at the people around you—family, friends or people you work with.

Being critical of others is just as harmful as the critic that beats you up. Either way it goes, the voice is a negative force that has a sole purpose to destroy your confidence and compassion.

Focus on your awareness of **self-criticism.**

One practice is to soften this voice. Treat your negative voices with compassion. Don't talk back or get angry. This inner voice is still you, it is just the uglier, angrier version of you. It can be talked down with gentle persuasion and compassion. It is the child or young adult that is on the fence, ready to defend.

Directed criticism

When feeling inadequate, you go on the attack and look for the "worst traits" in people. This leads to judgment and tearing apart another person's reputation.

The Seven-Day Anti-Criticism Challenge

Criticism is a destructive form of negativity. Delivered in the wrong pitch or manner, it can destroy someone's confidence and leave them emotionally "crippled" for life. If you grew up in an environment that weighed heavily on criticism to succeed, you know the damage that this can cause. I recommend you take the Seven-Day Anti-Criticism Challenge.

Make a challenge with yourself that you are not going to criticize or say anything negative about anyone, no matter what they do. This does not mean you have to be passive and just accept everything they do. Seek another way to express your feelings that is not along the lines of criticism or judgment.

Several months ago, I challenged myself to do this. Within the first few days, I did not make it past a few hours without making a comment, opinion, or criticizing someone. I intentionally looked for defects in others and set out to expose them.

Years of this repetitive behavior led to a bad habit of complaining and a deep sadness I was living with after realizing how critical I actually was.

To combat this, I started practicing the anti-complaining strategy. It works like this: you have to make a contract with yourself that you will not say anything that damages another person's reputation. This includes everything from backstabbing to sarcastic remarks aimed at tearing down another person's reputation.

This form of negative attacking is extremely damaging, not only to the person you are doing it to but also to yourself. It is a form of hidden self-sabotage. It may be so habitual that you're not aware you are doing it.

Try this for seven days. You will fail at this if self-criticism or directed criticism is a habit. When you fail, make note of the date and time. Start again right away. Start with a new slate. Don't wait for the next day to roll around.

Once I stopped, everything changed — my perspective, my mood, and my desire to be right. It also eliminated my need to counterattack, which was one of my core negative coping strategies.

Action Steps

For the next seven days, you are going to make a promise to yourself not to criticize or condemn yourself or others in any way. This will require a great amount of self-discipline. And you will likely fail many times. But that is okay. The goal is to eliminate your need to criticize yourself or others.

Once you hit the 7-day mark, your next challenge is to hit 14 days. Imagine your level of compassion for yourself and other human beings when you hit this mark.

220 · SCOTT ALLAN

I recommend using a calendar to mark off every day you succeeded without having a critical thought about yourself or another person. By marking it down on a calendar, you can see the progress you are making.

The 2-Way Mirror Strategy

This is a great technique for calming anxiety and lowering your nervousness so that you can function and be yourself. Spend a few minutes with yourself in front of a mirror. It may feel uncomfortable at first, but after a few times, it will become a habit. Do this for just a few minutes in the morning. To save time, do it while styling your hair, shaving, putting on makeup, or brushing your teeth.

Talk positively to yourself. Do not criticize or condemn anything about yourself. Talk to yourself as if you were talking to a best friend. Be the best friend you have ever had. Give yourself positive advice.

Look yourself in the eye and just give yourself advice as if you would give it to someone you care about. Do this technique for ten minutes a day, first thing in the morning. It builds your confidence, centers your thoughts, and enhances self-compassion.

Here is what you could do:

Talk about an achievement you recently had. Praise yourself and give credit for something you recently did. This does not have to be an over-the-top achievement. Just keep it simple.

Talk about the great day you are going to have. Pump yourself up by talking about all the great things you are going to do today. Will you spend time with friends, family, or your children? Will you do something fun that you have been looking forward to? The purpose of this is to get yourself into a positive frame of mind and to develop a healthy mindset for the day.

Talk about someone you love and admire. This is a great way to start feeling good about people again. Talk to yourself about the most important people in your life.

Talk about someone you have resentment toward. Just as it is important to talk about the people you love; now talk about someone you have a difficult relationship with. Think of one good thing you can say about this person. Imagine he or she is staring back at you as you are having a conversation. This strategy removes the negative energy that builds up when you have to deal with difficult people.

The Substitution Technique for Lasting Change

In order to generate a mindful mind and bring your compassion to the surface, you can apply the substitution technique to reinforce positive self-talk.

It works like this:

If you are in the habit of talking down (self-criticizing) about yourself, you can turn this around using this replacement technique. Instead of talking negatively to yourself with "I suck at this", you could say, "I am now learning how to do this better."

The objective is to reinforce your thoughts with positive anecdotes and words that support you. Begin by replacing the negative thoughts you have with empowering thoughts. Substitute your default belief that you're no good with a belief that empowers you.

Do not accept any thought that builds on your doubt and fear. Instead of "I am no good", you say, "I am great"; "My life sucks" is substituted with "I am grateful to have everything that I do." You can make a list of your gratitude and refer to this list when doing this activity.

Now, use the substitution technique for replacing:

- Harmful, negative words with positive expressions. You can include affirmations that work amazingly well when it comes to forming a positive mindset.

- Worry-based, fearful thinking with positive images that encourage immediate action. This will move you closer toward your objectives.

- Destructive bad habits with good habits that lead to positive results while creating a better process for doing things.

The Substitution Technique in Action

When you catch yourself criticizing either yourself or others, you can replace this behavior with the opposite action. Instead of criticizing and judging, speak well of others. Build up their reputation. Stop yourself immediately and change this behavior from condemning and verbal criticism to praising the reputation of others.

Challenge yourself to do this for one week. Make it a conscious habit to convert all negative actions, behaviors, and conversations into a stream of positive conviction.

Tell yourself, "I am so happy you're here."

Tell others, "You are great! I am so happy to have you in my life!"

Self-compassion and compassion towards others are a powerful gift. I want you to embrace this gift and make it a part of you. This isn't a random act of kindness but something to practice every minute of the day. When you find your compassion slipping away and need to reconnect, meditation and practicing mindfulness will bring you back to the center.

Failure Is the Way

(Your Eight-Step Action Plan for Handling Setbacks)

> *When you fall down, focus on the solution, not the problem. You might quit or fail 100 times. Keep that clear picture of where you want to be.*
>
> **– David Goggins,** United States Navy SEAL and bestselling author of *Can't Hurt Me*

My friend David Harper was convinced he had everything. A steady job that paid six figures a year, a wealthy 401k plan, and a home that he had worked hard to build.

One day, he showed up at his corporate job and was called into an immediate meeting. They were "restructuring," and in business what that means is, "We are firing a bunch of people we don't want to pay anymore."

Now, David had no job. He started searching for another job right away with a family at home and lives to support. But job offers were scarce and were nowhere near as good as what he had with his previous job. He turned down three offers because they couldn't match the great benefits and salary at his last job.

Six months later, he was still without work, savings were running out, and nothing was matching his expectations. When he met up with a life coach, she said, "You're comparing everything to what you had. You need to let that go and move on. You may have lost a good thing, but that wasn't your fault. Starting over is okay. And that is what you may have to do because you have unrealistic expectations. Take a step back. Take a job that can get you back on your feet. Then the pressure is off."

David had a setback he was never expecting; feeling (and believing) he was secure in his job he had never considered himself to be in a situation where he would feel like a big failure. He blamed the economy and he blamed his previous managers for not watching his back.

"But the blame has to end," she said. "Your excuses are mounting up and you're not on a path that is moving forward when you try to recreate what you lost. You might have to start again, but you have to start somewhere."

That is what David did. He took another job that paid much less, sold his home, and moved into something more affordable. Two years later, through the contacts and experience in the new job he took, he was hired by another company that made him a senior partner.

David worked through the setback because he stopped blaming everyone, talked with people he trusted who could help, and killed the negativity that was holding him back, and it worked out. He navigated through the one of the stormiest seasons in his life, persevered, and recovered.

When setbacks try to *kill your future*, you have to be ready to make a great comeback.

The Danger of Setbacks

Failing is the risk you commit to taking when you work consistently towards a goal, commit to building your dream, structuring a new business, negotiating a big contract, or fail forward with your vision of a life that you want to own.

But nothing is easy. There are hard times and challenging days ahead. You will gain and lose ground. You will win and lose your battles. People you work with will disappoint and when you think you have lots of support, suddenly find yourself alone with nobody to back you.

As David Goggins said, "*When you fall down, focus on the solution, not the problem. You might quit or fail 100 times. Keep that clear picture of where you want to be.*"

The vision of where you are going is your laser-focus. If you are thinking about giving up, take yourself back to your vision of what brought you this far to begin with. You're carrying a dream inside, and failing big is how you will make it happen.

What do you do after suffering a blow that knocks you back?

- The business deal you've been working on for seven months goes bust.

- The company you just started working for goes bankrupt right after you signed the papers on your new mortgage.

- Three months after getting married, the love of your life runs off with someone else.

- Your business partner doesn't show up for work one day. It turns out he ran off with your executive ... taking your money with him.

- Two months before competing in the Olympics, you twist your ankle in a race.

Yes, it does suck at times. Failure, extreme setbacks, and unexpected events happen when you least expect any of it. One day your world is a beautiful thing, and the next day tragedy strikes. But, as I have been teaching throughout this book, many of life's misfortunes have less to do with you and more to do with the waves of the world as it shifts through rapid change.

There is no such thing as a perfect plan. It's what you do when the plan goes AWOL.

In times of duress you ask yourself, "Now what am I going to do? Who do I trust? What's left after this?"

You have to be careful not to reframe the moment with a negative perspective. If you make yourself a victim, the actions you take will be to garner sympathy and contribute to making you weak.

A weakness is like a dent in your armor, and your enemies will sense this and move in for the kill. Stay strong and ask the right questions.

"What would be my best course of action to move past this?"

You must focus on the next step. "What's next?"

You have been hit hard by a setback and you're on the floor. What do you do? Stay down or get up?

When you suffer a setback, it is a natural inclination to feel like a loser. You lost and now you think you can't recover. The climb back is too far, and you've been through so much.

When you get knocked down the ladder, you have two choices and you need to choose one: 1. Get off the ladder altogether and give up on the climb. 2. Keep on climbing. Or you might find another ladder to climb. But whatever your choice is, if you give up on the path to ascension, you will surrender your default habit when things go bad.

You might fall back into your victim mindset of, "Life is not fair." Who said it was fair? Playing fair is for people who expect everything to go the way they want it to. It doesn't happen that way. Be sure your expectations are true and realistic.

Johnny Cash had it right when he said:

"You build on failure. You use it as a stepping stone. Close the door on the past. You don't try to forget the mistakes, but you don't dwell on it. You don't let it have any of your energy, or any of your time, or any of your space."

What is a realistic expectation? That life isn't fair, and as Scott Peck says in the opening line to his book *The Road Less Travelled*, "Life is difficult."

It isn't anything else but that. It doesn't say that life is easy, and you'll have the occasional bad day. **Life is difficult**, and if you're having an easy life, maybe you aren't pushing hard enough. Nothing should be easy when failing fast and driving your energy ahead to get to the next plateau. The climb up the mountain is the struggle; the peak is your victory, but it never ends there. You are never finished pushing on to that next phase.

The easy path is for the lazy who expect all things to work out in their favor. When it doesn't go according to plan, then what do you do?

Complain. Blame. Criticize.

This path is for failures committed to failing hard and never making forward progress. Do you stand at the base of the mountain thinking about what it would be like at the top or are you putting in the work to get there?

There will always be setbacks and challenges that come in many forms: Health issues, financial shortages, or relationship problems.

Here is a list of several common setbacks you could run up against. How you handle each setback is different, but our steps to dealing with it can be applied to any of these.

Nine Common Reasons for Setbacks

Betrayal: Your business partner steals your business and runs off with your best customer.

Loss: You lose someone close to you who was a huge influence in your life.

Distractions: You can reduce this setback by clearing away the distractions surrounding you. This can be handled with a change in your environment. Focus your mind on your work. Catch yourself when being pulled towards this distraction.

Self-sabotage: You set yourself up for failure by doing things that destroy your success before you get there.

Blind spots: You didn't see the curve ball coming because you took your attention off the weak link in your business/life.

Motivation: You've lost all energy and momentum for getting things done. Don't worry, this is an easy fix.

Lack of Knowledge/Information: Is there a skill you failed to master that resulted in your setback? Identify what that is and learn it.

Financial Trouble: That loan you are counting on just went through ... and then it fell through.

Damaging Self-Talk: You are not always aware of this, but beneath the surface is a voice that speaks to you when you are busy doing everything else. This voice can be a gentle, comforting soul or a mad, angry hatter. You control this voice but only when you recognize it's there.

The purpose for having a system to deal with your setbacks is so you can prepare better for upcoming obstacles. We can't avoid running into barriers, but we can prepare for the worst. Knowing what to do, and being confident in your ability to act, is key. No matter what happens, you are a survivor and a thriver.

> *"Always bear in mind that your own resolution to succeed is more important than any other."*

Here are the eight steps for dealing with setbacks:

(1). Do nothing. Step back. Breathe deeply. Absorb what has happened.

Take a day or two to absorb what happened. You'll be tempted to beat yourself up. Your internal critical monster decides to speak up. But after that, push aside your emotional carnage and come to terms with what happened.

Regardless whose fault it is, that doesn't matter. Do you want to focus on fault or solutions? During this phase I will meditate, focus on my thoughts, or listen to relaxing music to calm my mind.

(2). Accept what happened. Welcome the situation.

You lost money. Failed to get the contract. Gained weight instead of losing it. Someone you love left you.

Okay, now that you've had time to think it through, put an end to wishing you could change this. One of the first things we do when going through failure is fall into the trap of, "If only I had…"

Here is what that looks like:

"If only I had…"

- Been kinder, she would have stayed.

- Been smarter, I could have made it work

- Been available, I would have seen it coming.

You want to succeed. Everyone does. But when you don't, be welcoming to the situation even when it isn't in your favor. You might be in a bad spot. You lost everything. The situation appears hopeless. Don't rush ahead and make foolish decisions right away. When you are feeling frightened and panicked, that is when you need to step back, assess where you're at, and take intentional action to move towards the place you want to be.

You are not going to undo the past. You can only influence tomorrow by making a decision in the now and taking intentional action.

Right now, welcome this experience into your life and move ahead with the next step that is…

(3). Shake off your feelings of failure. Stop dwelling.

The pity train has to end. If you're still on it after a week, you need to get moving. While not every situation is going to require this step, you could be going through a mourning process or stuck. If you are dwelling on the mistakes you made and how you could have done this better, that is good.

Identify what that is and implement your next action according to your plan. You don't want to repeat the same mistakes, so knowing what you could do in the future to improve will accelerate your learning curve. You always learn faster by recognizing the better approach.

Right now, make a short list of two or three things you didn't do that you could implement in the future.

(4). Identify your #1 supporter and meet this person.

Do you have a coach or mentor? Is there someone you can talk to? This is an important step. You might be an introvert and rarely talk to anyone, like I can be, but in times of crisis or setbacks, you should talk it through with someone. This is going to be your first step towards forming a new action plan.

Years ago, when I was going through a difficult time, I had arranged to meet my mentor on a virtual one to one. In that brief 30-minute conversation I was filled with the courage and inspiration to get unstuck and move ahead with a plan of action.

Reflecting on this now, without that interaction, I could have spent months—or longer—spinning my wheels in confusion with a lack of confidence or clarity.

Right now, write down this person's name and a date by when you will meet them. Prepare a list of questions to ask and be open to the advice and suggestions they share.

(5). Accept NO excuses.

You know that internal monologue I keep talking about? It's going to fill up your head with all the reasons why you should retreat. Take no excuses. This is your mind filling your thoughts with lies.

Your excuses sound like this:

- "I'll try this again sometime when I'm not so tired."

- "It was never meant to be."

- "I'll wait until I have enough money, more resources, more time…"

- "What will my friends/peers/parents think?"

- "I don't have the energy for this anymore."

You get the idea. The excuses you tell yourself is your mind's way of deceiving you. Excuses are filled with the sounds of self-pity and victim mentality reasoning. Kill your excuses as soon as they crop up. Kill them before they kill you.

Here is what David Goggins, the bestselling author of *Can't Hurt Me*, says about excuses:

"Stop making excuses. Stop being a victim. Take personal responsibility. Hold yourself accountable. Get comfortable with the uncomfortable. And finally, make your dreams come true."

Right now, write down the excuses you are telling yourself. If you're like me, you have a list of them that appear when everything is falling apart. Call these excuses out when they appear. Diminish the power of your excuses by taking a mental "hammer" and pounding them down to nothing.

(6). Create a plan. Ask yourself, "What's next?"

This is the time to get unstuck and move. You are taking a step ahead and a step up into action. Put the wheels in motion. Make a list of first action steps. What are they? Now take the action step you can do today and get to work. Block off time if you have to. Commit one hour to nothing but working your plan. Don't rely on anyone to show up to rescue you.

When you fail at something and you're the only one standing with nobody else to lean on, you must support yourself. You can ask for help later, but don't wait for a rescue boat that may never come.

Ask yourself: "What can I do right now?"

Ask yourself, "What's next?" Do that action. After you check this off your list, ask yourself again: "What's next?" You will never be stuck if you continue to move yourself in this direction: Ask. Act. Refresh and repeat.

Right now, identify the one thing you can do today. It could be as simple as sending an email to someone or just making the right decision. But do something. Avoid procrastinating and waiting for the situation to fix itself if there is action you can take.

(7). Focus on the Controllable(s).

So many events are beyond your control. There isn't much you can do when people make their own decisions that impact your life. But you can control how you react to it.

Control what you can and focus on the situation you can influence. Remember earlier when I said life isn't fair? No moaning or complaining. It isn't fair, it never was, and it never will be.

This is the one thing nobody can ever take away from you: The freedom to take action and choose your attitude in any circumstance. If your business plummets because the economy crashed and people ran with their money, moaning about the economy and the unfairness of life won't change anything. What can you influence in this situation?

How you decide to scale your business. Communicating with your customers. Invest your time in adding value to a situation instead of letting it rob you of energy. Many people get depressed when they focus on the event out of their control instead of the decision-making power they have.

Right now, focus on your controllable(s) and get to work.

(8). Recite your Fail Big mantra: "I am strong because I am challenged."

It is the challenges of setbacks that form physical and mental toughness. Without them, you're like a new shield that has never had the taste of battle. You can overcome and win by reciting words of power that lift you up. This will silence the internal voices of shame and uncertainty. The ego doesn't like to fail, and it will let you know that.

Keep a list of your favorite positivity quotes on hand. Your mantra that you use to get through those *Fail Big* times, you want to use that now. You can harness your internal power by speaking to it in your own words instead of the words it tries to feed you.

Right now, write down on paper your absolute favorite positivity quote or mantra. Make a short list of quotes and read this out loud for five minutes in the morning. Read your mantra again before sleep.

This IS Not the END

It's never the end. If you catch yourself saying, "Now it's over," get a grip on your reality. A failure is never the end game. It is the step towards something else. The end is for people who are giving up and accepting this as the final outcome. If your dream is to start a business and that business fails, will you give up and go back to your old job you hate? If you do, then it really is the end.

Right now, tell yourself, "This is not the end. It isn't over until I say it is."

Accept No Excuses

This is what failing is all about. It isn't a simple process of giving up and trying the next best thing. If you are working towards a dream or goal that can change the course of your life, dealing with the setbacks on the way is the journey.

You might get frustrated or disappointed, but nothing can compare to the failure you'll have if you don't do something and push ahead. You've got this. Refer to this chapter anytime you have a setback. Know that you will make mistakes, you will fail, and you will disappoint yourself at times. But all of this is temporary. Setbacks will happen, but if you want to fail fast, you have to act with intention.

A Fail Fast Philosophy
for Change

"I've come to believe that all my past failure and frustrations were actually laying the foundation for the understandings that have created the new level of living I now enjoy."

— **Tony Robbins,** bestselling author of
Unlimited Power

This is it. You are now ready to take on your Fail Big challenges. Remember that the knowledge, wisdom and strategies I shared with you in this book mean nothing if you are not going to take massive action.

A lack of action equals a lack of results. You have to do something, even if it means that you won't succeed the first, second, or third time. That is why we are here. To test the battleground. To do the things we once dreamed of doing but were held back by:

Fear.

Doubt.

Shortage of Confidence.

You can use this to your advantage. Your fear of not succeeding can push you to the edge of your limitations and then past it into a new zone of comfort. All things achieved can always be traced back to the initial decision to move forward.

At the beginning of every day, as you wake up to a new set of challenges and setbacks, how you want to live is defined in the moment. When something happens and people are looking to you to fix it, what will be your solution?

When you are stuck in making a decision that can affect your life and the lives of your family, how long will you take to decide? What are the risks and are you okay to accept these risks? Is the risk worth it if you succeed? What is the risk of not moving forward?

If you fall into a rut in your life—and we all do at some point—the rope you need to get out of it is right in front of you. Most people fail to recognize that and they are waiting for someone to throw them a lifeline. But you have the greatest lifeline of all: Willpower. Determination. Ambition. You don't need permission to break out of your prison. You just need to grab that rope and start climbing up towards a better freedom.

Too often in this life we get stuck. We stop growing. We slide down deeper into depression or remorse. Instead of failing big, we just keep failing. The road to success is not a destination but a combination of daily tasks engineered to drive you towards reaching a positive state of mind.

If you are in pain, what will you do to get out of it?

What are you willing to sacrifice today in order to live large tomorrow?

Who do you have to reach out to for help? Who do you have to let go if they are holding you back? What is the #1 task you have to do right now, no matter how small, to start the momentum train rolling forward?

A Vision for Reinvention

This book has taken on great significance, not because of the theme or approach to failing but because I encourage you to develop a vision of how you want your life to evolve. You don't have to take my advice as the only roadmap. I'm a teacher and a student, but you can decide the direction you want to take and how you want to grow and develop.

Starting Over: Failure Is Never Fatal

We now know that failure is the way to success. But what do you do if you worked your ass off, succeeded where others had failed, and, just as things started picking up for you, found yourself back at square one again ... starting over again.

Your success, for whatever reason, reverted back to a failure again. You went from rags to riches and back to rags. One minute you are embracing your life as a successful journey and the next left to begin again.

Can you imagine how frustrating that would be? Would you have the resilience to begin again? Would you be willing to tackle that same mountain again that made you a success in the first place? Or would you try something different?

Or would you give up?

I know you wouldn't throw in the towel after failing again, but this brings us to the lesson in this chapter, and I can best sum it up with a well-known quote you've probably heard before:

> *Success Is Never Final and Failure Never Fatal.*
> *It's Courage That Counts.*

It's Never Too Late for a New Beginning

It is easy (and natural) to get comfortable with our success. We can get comfortable with failure, too, but if you were content with your failing, you wouldn't be reading this book. So, let's just assume failing and not pushing forward with your goals is something that doesn't sit well with you. But when you achieve your victory, what happens then? Do you keep climbing, changing, and making your (company, life, children, situation) better?

Of course you do. But what many people overlook is that life and the situations we are constantly influenced by are always changing.

Think of everything moving like the tides of the great ocean, rising and falling and then occasionally being prone to a great storm that we have no control over. Most of the circumstances that are heaped at you from week to week have little to do with anything we did to influence them. The only thing you can influence is what you take direct action towards.

There are a lot of cases out there where people have found themselves in a desperate situation after years of living well, only to one day be at the bottom of the barrel again scraping together what they can to survive.

You can call this the fallen hero syndrome. The warrior rises out of the ashes of nothing, builds an empire with his hands, loses it years later, and then is left with the fateful decision...

Do I stage an attack to win back victory or cut my losses and do something else?

You can, in the midst of any crisis, choose to get up or stay down. Accepting your losses is one thing, but accepting fate is another.

Your success is not a permanent fixture. Everything is changing, evolving, erupting, and so much of it happens as we are going about our day. One day business and life is good, and the next day something shifts and we must roll with it. But we are not concerned with what we can't control. Why worry about the stuff beyond our reach?

Stay focused on the controllable. Influence what you can and let the rest move as it is.

Failing Towards Your Big Dream

What does it take for someone to live out their dreams?

It takes three things...

A vision for how to get there.

Consistent action to take you there.

Persistence to keep moving forward after you've arrived.

Success has nothing to do with luck or coincidence.

You succeed by showing up to play every day, especially the days when your mind screams for you to stop.

Never give in to your excuses.

Ask these questions of yourself…

How many shots does one have to take before becoming a candidate for the NBA?

How many hours spent writing bad material before someone like JK Rowling and Lawrence Sanders can create bestseller after bestseller?

How many decades spent failing in politics before someone like Lincoln becomes president?

How many cars did Ford make before he came up with the Model T?

How many times failing can someone recover from drug, alcohol or sexual addiction?

How many nights did Colonel Sanders spend sleeping in his car before finally getting an investor for his chicken recipe?

How many interviews did you go through before finding a job?

How many times did Walt Disney fail at business before finally making it?

When you break it down and study the consistent actions of super achievers who are successful, you can see the key steps/strategies they implemented that eventually led to a successful outcome.

Throughout the frustrations, failings and working late nights and weekends, entrepreneurs, creatives, or busy single parents can achieve anything they desire if they are willing to put in the work.

As we have discovered by reading *Fail Big*, there is one message, if you take anything from this book: **It is not what you gain by**

achieving your dreams but who you are becoming through reaching your goals.

It is not about luck or being in the right place at the right time but a deep knowing that, if you keep pushing forward, shooting straight for your dreams without giving into negative self-talk or the critics that feed doubt into your mindset, you can crush all obstacles in your way.

You become unstoppable. Failure is just a means of getting there.

You are ready for this.

You were born for this.

Fail your way to success and conquer the "Everest" of your dreams.

I'll see you there at the top.

Scott Allan

"We think of failing as the worst thing that can happen to us. But failing isn't the worst thing that can happen to you. Failing to take action towards your dreams is the real failure. The biggest failure of all? Knowing what your dream is and waiting for the day when you'll get up and do something about it. But by then, it's too late. The opportunities you said no to while you were waiting for that next boat to arrive are gone now."

— **Scott Allan**

Download this <u>Free Training</u> Guide—Built For Stealth: Key Principles for Building a Great Life

Available wherever <u>books</u>, <u>eBooks</u> and <u>audiobooks</u> are sold.

Books Change Lives.
Let's Change Yours Today.

Check out the complete
Bulletproof Mindset Mastery series here by Scott Allan.

Visit author.to/ScottAllanBooks or scan the QR Code below to
follow Scott Allan and stay up to date on future book releases

The **Rejection Free for Life**
Series Books

Begin Your Rejection Free Journey Today!
RejectionFreeBooks.com

Pathways to Mastery Series

Master Your Life One Book at a Time

Available where eBooks, books and
audiobooks are sold.

About Scott Allan

Scott Allan is an international bestselling author of 25+ books published in 7 languages in the area of personal growth and self-development. He is the author of **Fail Big**, **Undefeated,** and **Do the Hard Things First**.

As a former corporate business trainer in Japan, and **Transformational Mindset Strategist**, Scott has invested over 10,000 hours of research and instructional coaching into the areas of self-mastery and leadership training.

With an unrelenting passion for teaching, building critical life skills, and inspiring people around the world to take charge of their lives, Scott Allan is committed to a path of **constant and never-ending self-improvement**.

Many of the success strategies and self-empowerment material that is reinventing lives around the world evolves from Scott Allan's 20 years of practice and teaching critical skills to corporate executives, individuals, and business owners.

You can connect with Scott at:

scottallan@scottallanpublishing.com

Visit author.to/ScottAllanBooks to stay up to date on future book releases.

Scott Allan

"Master Your Life One Book at a Time."

<u>Subscribe</u> to the weekly newsletter for actionable content and updates on future book releases from Scott Allan.